"I have greatly admired Neeti Dewan's drive and achievements, and have wondered at her ability to maintain a sparkling personality and positive attitude in today's stressful environment. This book is a roadmap we can all use on our quest for personal fulfillment and success."

— Jane Adam, General Manager, Global Tax & Trade, NISSAN MOTOR CO., LTD.

"This book deserves to be in the hands of every employee! It challenges you to new heights and provides practical principles you can put to use immediately."

— A. Allen Arroyo, Corporate Controller, IHOP Corp.

"A reading of Ms. Dewan's book explains the source of her positive energy and balance. This book provides the reader basics and subtleties needed to obtain work life balance and excel in every endeavor a person may encounter in his or her life; a definite must read for the busy professional."

— Yosef Z. Barber, Corporate Auditor SEC Compliance, CKE Restaurants.

"I love it when someone from another culture comes to the U.S. and views the world with another perspective... one we may not think of. Use this book with that in mind: some of these ideas, thoughts, and reflections you already know, and Neeti Dewan fleshes them out and brings them to life. The one that stays with me is "You have many roles in life, and don't let one role overpower the other. You must have balance in life, but strive to be the best that you can be in each of your roles, no matter what you are doing."

> — Bernadine Bednarz, Project Manager, Southern
> California Committee for the Olympic Games.

"Among circles of women business owners, Neeti Dewan has been known for years for her refreshing and motivating presence. Whether as a business owner herself, author, board-member, friend, or financial advisor, she has been a role model. Now we know her real secret to energy and a full life as shared in her book. This is the antidote for stress we've all been seeking."

> — Betsy Berkhemer-Credaire, Past California
> President, NAWBO and President, Berkhemer
> Clayton, Inc.

"Neeti Dewan's book nicely brings out the technique to increase focus and concentration within a few seconds. This is an absolute necessity for corporate executives of present era. The essential message put forth in this excellent literary piece of work is that meditation, even for a very short duration, may be enough to help you perform at the highest levels at work, and lead an active and balanced life outside of work. A MUST READ for all corporate executives."

> — Anurag Bist, Ph.D., Founder & CEO, Moxair, Inc.
> and Founder, VxTel.

"How do you excel in life, do YOUR best, and still remain centered on OTHERS in order to work together to improve your community and your world? This book provides answers you can apply to your own life's success in a way that will create positive energy for others!"

> – Cindy Burrell, VP Corporate Relations,
> Boardroom Bound.

"Neeti Dewan's powerful book is a MUST-READ for all business leaders who want to win in today's GLOBAL economy."

> – Deepak Chopra, CEO, OSI Systems.

"With a keen wit and lovely sense of self, Neeti Dewan shares stories from her life with a purpose. Neeti is truly a guide...a woman with a desire to share and to help others live better lives."

> – Patty DeDominic, Founder, PDQ Careers,
> Inc., Past Board Chair, LA Area Chamber of
> Commerce.

"Neeti Dewan's book is an easy and entertaining read! I wholeheartedly agree with her that we must focus on being the best at whatever we do, not be driven by a paycheck, and live our lives with a purposeful focus on others at all times."

> – Carl S. DiNicola, Partner, Ernst & Young.

"Beautifully written, Neeti Dewan's book is full of business and personal leadership strategies which can be used by anyone to become an effective leader."

> – Tracey Doi, Group Vice President, Chief Financial
> Officer, Toyota Motor Sales, USA., Inc.

"Neeti Dewan sets forth an approach to life that is energizing, fulfilling and empowering. A compelling story teller, Dewan shares the intimate stories of her life growing up in India and in the United States to illustrate the 12 "powers" or principles to achieve a balanced and successful life. The Executive Yogi can teach you a path to success or help you correct your course on your own path to success."

> – Robert A. Earnest, Director, Legal & Tax, Superior Industries.

"Stress is a necessary part of being a powerful leader. But knowing how to manage it and create balance is always tough. Ms. Dewan's wonderful book has insights and practical advice that make it the "must read" book! Power comes from within and she knows how to fuel the source."

> – Renee Fraser, Ph.D., President and CEO, Fraser Communications, Past President of NAWBO-LA Enterprise Institute.

"Neeti Dewan's positive impact and proven success in each and every position she has had in her career provides instant credibility for this powerful book. It is a must read for anyone looking to win in the global workplace . . . and in life."

> – Greg Hunt, Founding Partner in the executive search firm of Kaufman Hunt.

"Neeti Dewan brings passion, energy, and intensity to everything she does. I am glad she has distilled some of this into a book that can be shared more broadly. Every reader of this book is bound to finish it having a better outlook on life."

> – Kimberly Jones, National Director, PricewaterhouseCoopers Office of Diversity.

"As an executive having lived in and out of India, I found Ms. Dewan's book entertaining, informative, and packed full of practical insights! Neeti Dewan has written the ultimate book for overall success in life, and her principles have such universal application that they can be used by anyone, whether you live in the Western world or in the East — be it in business or in your personal life."

> – Rajesh R. Jumani, General Manager- Middle East, Tata Interactive Systems.

"Neeti's enthusiastic approach to a balanced life is most refreshing and offers sound advice to everyone dealing with the demanding requirements of both personal life and career that are such an entrenched part of our world today."

> – Larry G. Kinney, Chief Financial Officer, Galls, an ARAMARK company, LLC.

"Neeti Dewan has a creative and powerful approach as it relates to Life-Work Effectiveness. From Executive to Yogi in Sixty Seconds is a must read for all business professionals."

> – Nicholas Longo, Principal, Ryan & Company.

"Neeti Dewan's art of meaningful storytelling holds us enthralled as she shares the important message of living a balanced life, no matter what our position in life. She leaves us with a sense of optimism, hope, and joy."

> – Andrea March, Co-Founder, Women's Leadership Exchange.

"In this insightful book, you will learn how to master powers that will make you and your company stars in the new global economy."

> – Bobbi McKenna, Publisher of Givingyouavoice.com Internet Magazine and Global Business and Branding Consultant.

"In this book, Neeti Dewan shares the secrets she has used to bring passion to a very balanced life. A must read."

> – David Michaelson, Vice President, Finance, Aramark Uniform Services, Inc.

"This book is an invaluable and refreshing look on life. Neeti Dewan inspires us to be the best we can be. She proves that you truly can have it all without sacrificing relationships, both personal and business."

> – Mary B. Mullin, CFP®, CIMA®, Wealth Management Advisor.

"Back to basics insightful reading!"

> – Ash Pradhan, Vice President, IT, Aramark Uniform Services, Inc.

"From Executive to Yogi in Sixty Seconds is a tool that Corporate America has been waiting for to help motivate and retain its best employees."

– Thomas Pucci, Partner, PricewaterhouseCoopers.

"Thanks to Neeti Dewan, you don't have to travel to an ashram in India to learn the secrets of a yogi. This book will transform the thinking of employers and employees alike. Her Executive Yogi Principles will drive YOU to extraordinary excellence in YOUR career, ALLOW YOU TO achieve better productivity and profitability, and at the same time help retain a motivated workforce."

– Jim Rohrbach, Success Skills Coach, Successskills. com

"Great Insight! Neeti's personal stories really bring the concepts home!"

– Lynda J. Roth, CEO, LJR Consulting Services, Inc.

"Personal, entertaining, and full of wisdom, whether in business or life in general, Neeti Dewan has given all of us a sage companion for our own travels through life. Thanks!"

– John Samore, Jr., Partner (Retired), Arthur Andersen.

"In her delightful voice, Neeti Dewan teaches us a Yogi's way to be very successful, AND very happy. An instant classic."

– Barbara Schell.

"In this delightful, easy to read book, Neeti Dewan shares practical ways in which we can find purpose in the work we do, bringing contagious contentment into the workforce and our lives. Ms. Dewan's philosophical understanding of East and West brings new meaning to the word Globalization. Great gift for co-workers and friends."

— Patty Schlee, Vice President, Senior Financial Advisor, UnionBanc Investment Service.

"Neeti Dewan is a brave, focused and caring practitioner of the art of living. Her new book gives great insight into a balanced productive path to success in business and in life. It is a practical step-by-step guide to applying techniques to clarify thinking and to achieve calm decisiveness."

— Rochelle Schneider, Attorney at Law, RJS Legal and Business Consulting, Past President NAWBO-OC.

"Ms. Dewan is truly a visionary. As an executive based in India, I find tremendous wealth of knowledge in her book that can be used by people in either the East or West to propel themselves to heights of achievement in their personal & business life. But more importantly, her book provides a roadmap for achieving a deep sense of contentment and joy in this fast-paced global world."

— Vijay K. Sharma, Managing Director, Amtek India Limited.

"Neeti Dewan, a top performer in a highly demanding profession, has managed to perform at the highest levels while maintaining an active and balanced life outside of work. In this book, you will learn how to stay on top of your game without sacrificing what is important in life."

– David Sniezko, Partner, Ernst & Young.

"Words of wisdom from an experienced and highly accomplished professional who has excelled in her field and has penned her expertise and ideas fit for present day management gurus. Ms. Dewan's principles are sure to benefit the present day managers and business leaders."

– Hans Raj Sood, Founder & Senior Partner, Sood & Company, chartered Accountant.

"Neeti Dewan is that rare individual who meets head-on all the challenges of a demanding career, motherhood and a strong commitment to her community, and does it all with a contagious enthusiasm. Read her book to discover some of her many secrets as to how she manages to accomplish all that she does."

– William Spina, Director of Taxes, DIRECTV.

"With the demands of the global marketplace which emphasizes staying agile and current to stay competitive, Neeti Dewan's book not only makes sense, but is a MUST READ to prevent yourself from burning out and losing perspective on what is really important in your life."

– Neil Stevens, Managing Director Woodland Hills, RESOURCES GLOBAL PROFESSIONALS.

FROM EXECUTIVE TO YOGI
IN
60 SECONDS

FROM EXECUTIVE TO YOGI
IN
60 SECONDS

A Revolutionary Approach to Increasing
Productivity, Profitability, and Personal Efficiency

BY

NEETI DEWAN
The Executive Yogi™

Everest Hall Press
Nevada

Library of Congress Cataloging-in-Publication Data
Dewan, Neeti
From Executive to Yogi in 60 Seconds / by Neeti Dewan – 1st Everest Hall Press ed.
Library of Congress Control Number: 2006922821

ISBN 0-9778468-0-6 (hardcover)

1. Leadership 2. Career 3. Success In Business 4. Personal Development
I. Title

Printed in the United States of America

DEDICATION

This book is dedicated to

My husband Al —

My soul mate and my best friend.

Without his

support, this book would have remained just a

dream.

DISCLAIMER LICENSE

This book is designed to provide the reader with information on success-building systems that the author has used successfully. The purpose of this book is to educate and entertain. Neither the author nor the publisher is engaged in providing legal, accounting, health, medical, or other professional services. The author and the publisher are not aware of the specific legal, accounting, health, or professional needs of the reader.

Questions related to specific tax, legal, real estate, accounting, career, or health issues, or other needs of the reader should be addressed to practicing members of those professions. Every effort has been made to make this book as accurate as possible. However, there may be errors, both typographical, and in content. The authors and the publisher specifically disclaim any liability, loss, or risk, personal or otherwise, incurred as a consequence, direct or indirect, in the use of and application of any of the techniques or contents of this book. This publication is copyrighted. The buyer is given a limited license to use its contents for his or her personal use. This book is sold to you, the buyer, with the agreement that your purchase entitles you to a non-exclusive right to use this book and the material contained herein for personal educational use. You agree that you will not copy or reproduce materials in any form and that you will not lease, loan, sell, or otherwise make them available to third parties or any others.

ACKNOWLEDGEMENTS

Bobbi McKenna, a Global Business Branding and Communications consultant, deserves my heartfelt thanks for her insights and guidance. She is the BEST at what she does!!!

My friends Anita Sniezko, Amanda Todd, Donna McIntyre, Monisha David, and Carolyn Hatfield who assisted me in the early stages of the book.

The Sodhi Family, my uncle and aunt, who sponsored my family to come to the U.S. They made it possible for me to explore the boundless opportunities this country has to offer. India's culture and economy shaped my early life. The United States provided the arena where I have been able to combine the values and genius of both countries.

My co-workers and the wonderful mentors, I've encountered throughout my career. Their vitality, dynamism, and professionalism have touched my psyche and shaped me into the person I am today. They have all — in one way or another — provided education, motivation, and inspiration.

My grandparents who laid the foundation for this book; my parents, whom I can never thank enough for what they provided – wisdom and a loving, secure home; my brother, with whom I spent a lively and joy-filled childhood; my mother and my mother-in-law (my two role models); and all the members of my husband's family who have enriched my life incredibly.

CONTENTS

INTRODUCTION

INTRODUCTION

What is an Executive Yogi?

- An Executive is thought of as a corporate officer or manager in a business or organization.

- A Yogi is a person who seeks development thru the integration and balance of body, mind, and spirit.

- An Executive Yogi™ is a specialist in the art of overall life success through the integration of business and personal development.

Think of it this way:

An executive's goal is to maximize the economic development of a business or organization and a yogi's goal is to maximize the development of the inner self.

Although these two goals — organizational

development and individual self-development
— are sometimes thought of as separate, I
believe that they are, in fact, inextricably inter-
twined.

As we develop the qualities of body,
mind, and spirit, we begin to achieve greater
control over our organizational and business
life as well.

You may be wondering how I came to
combine the term Executive with the term
Yogi. After all, they seem — at first glance
— to be contradictory, or even antagonistic,
concepts.

It happened like this:

I was born in India in Agra, the city that
is home to the Taj Mahal. My early life was
spent in India where I was brought up in the
ways of the yogi. As a teen, I came to the
United States where I was educated in business, becoming a CPA.

I have been fortunate enough to be able
to achieve professional excellence working
for some of the most prestigious companies
in the world and personal excellence in my
home, family, and friendships.

For several years, friends and colleagues have been urging me to share my secrets by writing a book.

A little over a year ago, I was talking with my friend and colleague Bobbi McKenna, who is a Global Business and Branding Consultant. In our first session together, she came up with the idea of The Executive Yogi™. As soon as I heard the words, I realized that they perfectly describe my approach to life, and that I could teach the principles behind them to others.

I believe that you can use these principles to help you:

- Rise to the top of your profession.

- Increase your productivity.

- Create financial security.

- Enhance your personal life.

- Develop more fulfilling relationships with your family and friends.

- Build a stronger body, mind, and spirit.

- Attain a new level of joy, contentment, and serenity.

CHAPTER ONE

"The Power Of The Yogi"

CHAPTER ONE

"The Power Of The Yogi"

A yogi has power, but this power is not in the fist nor is it in words.

This power comes from the depths of the mind, heart, and soul.

It's not brutish power, but rather it's a way of living that empowers us to have clarity about what is important in our lives through self-knowledge.

We do not have to look externally for this power.

It comes from within through introspection and discipline.

It is easy for us to connect with and bring forth.

New Delhi, India:

It is a hot steamy day when I am intro-
duced to the power of a yogi for the first
time. I am clinging to my mom as she
weaves through the busy local bazaar. She
is making her way through a maze of what
seem – to my child's eyes – like a million
people, all colliding into each other like
bumper cars at a carnival.

Vendors are shouting loudly as they
hawk their clay items, hand-made jewelry,
and rainbow-colored scarves while customers bark back the price they are willing
to pay (which is usually half of the asking
price).

A fruit vendor is trying to convince pe-
destrians that his fresh watermelons, papa-
yas, and mangoes are the best in the world
while a milkman is extolling the qualities of
the milk he is selling. Only a few minutes
earlier, I'd seen this very same milkman pour

water from the community water faucet into his milk containers. The original ten liters has thus been transformed into thirteen liters of milk (and low fat milk at that).

"Cling, Clang, Cling!"

I hear the loud bells from the nearby temple.

I see a crowd of beggars who have gathered around the temple. They hope to grab a few morsels of food from the temple-goers as they walk out with "prasad" (their offerings to the Lord).

Business people and shoppers loiter outside little storefronts drinking hot "chai" (tea) from their tall glasses and munching snacks they have purchased from vendors on the street.

Neither the throngs of sweaty people, nor the pounding sun is going to stop my mother from visiting the "yogi" she has come to see.

Suddenly, with no warning, someone begins to chant loudly. I look over my shoulder, and see my mother kneeling down in front of a man.

The man is clad from head-to-toe in nothing more than an orange loincloth. He has a yellow thread wrapped around his wrist like a bracelet, and sits with his legs folded in a "yoga" position. He stares straight ahead as if in deep thought.

He has a long shaggy beard, and his hair is pulled up into a bun. He also has a calm and luminous smile on his face which is hard to describe in words. He looks incredibly peaceful as he sits there, seemingly oblivious to the hard and hot cement. The only shade is provided by a sparse peepal tree, the leaves of which have long since left the branches on their autumnal journey.

People are sitting around the yogi. Some of them have their eyes closed and are chanting. Others have their eyes locked onto the yogi in utter admiration.

I stare at the yogi, trying to understand what he is doing: Why are so many people gathered around like bees buzzing around a flower?

This scrawny little man, who is the center of attention, appears to have no cares in the world. In what seems like a lifetime to me, I sit and wait for the yogi to speak to us.

I look out under my long lashes at the people who have gathered at the yogi's feet. They — in turn — continue to stare intently at the yogi.

My mother furrows her brow and gives me that look all mothers are good at and which says so much:

"Don't stare. It is rude. Sit still. Stop squirming."

Finally, the yogi lifts his head, and flashes a smile at everyone gathered around him. Sitting in that dusty town square with no possessions to call his own, this yogi has a look on his face that conveys immense contentment, happiness, and self-sufficiency.

He looks at everyone present around him, seeming to gaze into each set of eyes. He opens his mouth and lets a few eagerly-awaited words roll out.

"The world is within you!" — "Body and mind are but one." — "Seek and know your mind, and your heart will lead you to your destiny!"

I am mesmerized and feel that his dark, ocean-deep eyes are looking only at me — or "into me."

And then, he raises his right hand and gently places it over my head in the traditional Indian way of giving blessings, and speaks directly to me:

"My child, may life's true wealth be bestowed upon you. Seek and you shall find what your heart desires."

He continues to talk, and I become lost in his words. I dig my fingers deep into my mother's hand, holding her so tightly that she winces.

"What does he mean?" I wonder.

I scan his face for some insight, and he seems to notice my curiosity. He gives me a wide smile, and then goes back into his trance.

I didn't know it then, but his words would stay with me throughout my childhood and into my adulthood, right up to this very day.

- "Seek and know your mind, and your heart will lead you to your destiny!"

- "The world is within you!"

- "Body and mind are but one."

- "May Life's true wealth be bestowed upon you."

- "Seek and you shall find what your heart desires."

I don't sit in a town square with my legs folded in a yoga position, but in the years since that day so long ago when the Yogi spoke to me, I have applied the principles he shared with me to my own life.

These basic principles can be incorporated into our daily life with relative ease. We don't have to denounce our material pursuits, move to India, and climb to the summit of a Himalayan peak. These principles are not restricted to a time and space. They are universal and global.

We can do it from where we are RIGHT NOW. Let's begin!

At the end of each chapter, you'll notice the following words:

BREATHE

BE STILL

SMILE

Directions for use:

Whenever you feel that stress, anger, or frustration is interfering with your ability to function optimally or whenever you begin to feel disconnected, disjointed, and disorganized, take 60 seconds to create your own little mental oasis, and follow three simple steps:

- **Breathe** – With eyes closed, draw in positive energy, and exhale negative energy. (Slow inhalations and slow exhalations, 20 seconds.)

- **Be still** – Go to the center of your being. (Sitting perfectly still, 20 seconds.)

- **Smile** – Turn all negativity, both internal and external, into positive energy. (Eyes still closed, counting silently to 20 in your mind.)

You can follow these steps as often as once an hour or whenever you feel the need for it. This secret EXECUTIVE YOGI technique can help you maximize your performance and your sense of well-being. Regard this as your own secret SIXTY SECOND mental oasis.

CHAPTER TWO

"The Power Of Concentration"

CHAPTER TWO

"The Power Of Concentration"

Hulhundu (a lush green village in India):

My classmates and I are walking in a line, hand in hand, singing at the top of our lungs. We are full of high spirits. We are on our way to the annual school picnic.

Our school is located a half hour away from the city, right in the middle of a small village called Hulhundu. We have a tradition for picnics. Instead of traveling to another location, we simply march into the village near the school, and find a spot to host our picnic.

"Brown Girl in the ring, tra...la... la...la!" we sing. "Brown Girl in the ring, traaaaa...la...la...laaaaaaa!!"

We are singing this song by Boney M, the pop and disco group, as we tramp along the uneven village roads, resembling the untouched and crater-pocked surface of the moon.

Our maroon knee-length skirts and the ties with the school badge on them that reads "Sacred Heart School" are moving to the rhythm of our songs as our little legs march along the road.

I am holding a basketball in my hands, moving it to the rhythm of our song.

Curious villagers are poking their heads out of their thatched roof huts, and their children come running out, looking at us with amusement.

Suddenly, I hear a village elder shout:

"THE LUNATIC IS COMING!"

The man then scoops up his child with one of his dark brown arms, and rushes into his hut.

I turn my head sharply to one side and see the cause of his alarm thundering down the path directly toward us: a berserk gray elephant on a wild rampage.

"Lunatic" is an appropriate name for him. His muscles ripple on his dirt-smeared body. His eyes are burning red like the color of my favorite "red fire" nail polish.

He skids to a stop right in front of me. His red eyes lock with my cocoa brown eyes.

For a few seconds, we play a game of "who can stare the other down without blinking?"

I raise my skinny hairless arms up in the air, aiming the basketball in my hands right at his forehead.

I hear my teacher shrieking at me: "Don't be foolish, Neeti. Put that basketball down!"

She punctuates her words with one hand and hold's onto her nun's "head dress" with the other hand as the wind plays tug of war with her.

I hear the nun shouting at me to put down the basketball, but the ball is already in the air ready to make a three-pointer.

The crowd is cheering. The teachers are horrified. The girls are scattering.

I am still, focused, calm.

I watch as the basketball hits the elephant in the middle of his forehead, just at the spot where a "bindi" (red adornment dot) normally sits on an Indian woman.

The elephant thrusts his long trunk up in the air and bellows. The next instant he charges right at me. I turn and run as fast as I can. I run…and run…and run…too afraid to look back, but determined that I will not let "The Lunatic" catch up with me.

Suddenly, I don't hear the elephant's heavy footsteps thundering after me anymore. I slowly turn my head and see the elephant's master next to his side, calming him down with a treat of peanuts.

Panting and gasping for air, I head back to join my group.

Now, many years later, I still have a vivid memory of that elephant's eyes staring into mine. I can even remember how scared I was. Looking back, I'm a little surprised that I was so unwilling to back down. This was, after all, a five ton elephant that could have easily crushed me with one strike if he had decided to.

Somehow, even as a young child I had the courage to overcome fear. This is something we all must learn to do if we want to be successful in business and in life. We must not let other people stare us down or intimidate us because of their size, title, or position in life.

We must stand up for ourselves. The courage to do this comes from within.

I was able to find that kind of inner strength as a young child because of the early use of meditation. Meditation enabled me to connect with my inner self. It increased my focus and concentration, and it also weakened the pull of external distractions.

For our purposes in this book, let us define meditation as a concentrated stillness and a journey to the center, which brings calmness and clarity.

Meditation is actually quite easy to learn and can be practiced by anyone, almost anywhere. It does require practice over time until it becomes a habit.

Our minds are constantly bombarded with messages from the external world. Sometimes these messages burrow their way inside us, and we begin to hear them even within the confines of our own minds.

Our brains get tired. Even as we sleep, our brains slow down a little, but still continue to work by creating dreams and thoughts at an unconscious level.

Meditation allows the brain to unwind and relax while in a "purposeful conscious state." The mind withdraws from external activities and engages in "concentration."

Meditation allows us to control our minds and thus control our lives. Instead of a gazillion varied thoughts entering our heads from different sources, we learn to filter thoughts and use our trained minds as gatekeepers to keep out wasteful, unnecessary, and unhealthy thoughts.

Within our own minds, we learn to focus on the thoughts that are productive for our well being and for society as a whole.

We learn to function only out of a sense of goodness and good thoughts. Anything negative is filtered out, and nipped in the bud.

There are many different methods you can use to learn to meditate. You may want to learn meditation techniques from a meditation teacher, a CD, or a group class. The premise of most styles of meditation is similar: stillness.

As I begin my meditation routine each morning, I set an alarm for the allotted time. (Meditation can last anywhere from five minutes to an hour at a time.) Then I sit down on my yoga mat and tell myself that I am going to spend the next few minutes in "suspension."

I visualize myself staring into the bright and beady eyes of that rampaging elephant, which scared me as a child. I see my own eyes reflected in his eyes. The elephant's eyes provide a point of focus. The eyes help me turn internally into myself. Soon, my mind begins to relax just as my breathing becomes soft and shallow.

I am unaware of the passage of time, and when the alarm rings, I am pulled back into the material world. I bow my head and express my gratitude toward this wonderful life and the all-powerful brain that we have been given.

I am surrounded in peace. I feel refreshed and my brain starts flowing with creative ideas. I am now ready to start scripting my day and creating the life I want to experience.

You may be thinking, "I don't have time to meditate!"

That is a true statement to some extent. There is no time in our life to do anything unless we make time and write a script for it in the screenplay of our life.

Remember, you don't have to meditate for an hour to see results. Set a stopwatch, and begin by sitting still for two minutes. After a few weeks of this, try to set the timer for five minutes, and then work up to the amount of time that works for you and your schedule.

You don't have to meditate in the morning. You can do it anytime. You can take a few minutes to meditate during your lunch hour, break, or while waiting for a meeting to start. You can meditate while waiting for your child to arrive at the bus-stop from school, when you are feeding your children, or even for a few minutes as you sit in your car before heading home.

One popular method of meditation suggests using your own breath as a focal point. As you draw in a fresh breath of air, feel your chest move, focus on it, and concentrate on your inhalations and exhalations.

Random thoughts will enter your mind, but you can simply imagine yourself picking them up and throwing them out the window.

Continue this process and over time, you will notice that the frequency of random thoughts barraging your brain during meditation begins to subside. You will emerge from your period of meditation refreshed, re-energized and centered.

These are not the only benefits of meditation. For me, meditation also helps my mind stay clear and sharp. It also helps my body stay relaxed throughout the day. My blood pressure remains steady. I need less sleep.

In addition, some of my best ideas come to me during meditation. I do not know where the outpouring of these ideas comes from, but I do know that meditation seems to open up a pathway to a new frequency where ideas come rushing out from this "calm state."

The stillness of meditation stays with me throughout the day as I am more aware of my physical self, my actions, and their effects on others. I feel calmer, less reactive, and happier.

This serenity enables me to handle the pressures of life better.

BREATHE

BE STILL

SMILE

Directions for use:

Whenever you feel that stress, anger, or frustration is interfering with your ability to function optimally or whenever you begin to feel disconnected, disjointed, and disorganized, take 60 seconds to create your own little mental oasis, and follow three simple steps:

- **Breathe** – With eyes closed, draw in positive energy, and exhale negative energy. (Slow inhalations and slow exhalations, 20 seconds.)

- **Be still** – Go to the center of your being. (Sitting perfectly still, 20 seconds.)

- **Smile** – Turn all negativity, both internal and external, into positive energy. (Eyes still closed, counting silently to 20 in your mind.)

You can follow these steps as often as once an hour or whenever you feel the need for it. This secret EXECUTIVE YOGI technique can help you maximize your performance and your sense of well-being. Regard this as your own secret SIXTY SECOND mental oasis.

CHAPTER THREE

"The Power Of Work"

CHAPTER THREE

"The Power Of Work"

Many of us spend at least one third of our day at work. We should always aim to make that time productive. After all, if we are getting paid to get a task done, then our goal should be to bring value to our employer or business venture.

It is easy to be just "one of the employees" among many others. Our goal should always be to excel. Mentally focus on whatever task is at hand. When we are at work, that is where our unwavering focus must be.

I am a junior attending Granada Hills High School in California. I realize that in less than a year, I'll need a car to go to college. I don't want to ask my parents to pay for it.

They are already going to pay for my tuition. I therefore decide to find a part-time job. As I am leaving for my first day at the job, my dad sits me down, and puts an arm around me.

"Beta" (daughter), remember that when you are at work, you are out there representing not just yourself but also your parents and your community."

"Work harder than the person next to you."

"Always look for opportunities to improve your own work and your work place. Pitch in without being asked to."

His work ethic and diligence automatically earn him the respect of his colleagues.

He commands trust easily, and creates a work environment where people know that they must put in their full share and truly earn their paycheck. I think that is what he is trying to teach me as I begin my journey into the first real job.

My family finishes dinner and we are now sitting around the family room. The fan is on high and makes a squeaking noise each time it swings around to my side of the room.

My dad is wearing his traditional Indian casual lounge-outfit, called the "kurta-py-jama." (It is a loose white cotton shirt with matching pants pulled up with a drawstring.)

As he talks, he moves his head from side to side, as if his words of wisdom will move into my brain faster and deeper with each movement of his head. His hair is combed impeccably, but then again, that is not a major task. He only has a few pieces of hair around the sides. The top of his head is bald and shiny.

My dad, who is an engineer by profession, is a yogi in many ways. At his work he is known as Dewan "Sahib" (Mr. Dewan).

He continues to talk to me with fatherly concern and love shining in his dark brown eyes.

"Neeti, you must go to work each day with the mindset that you are there to work and contribute. Do not think about your paycheck or the car you want to buy with the money you earn. Your focus must be on being the very best at what you do. After a week of hard-earned work, when you finally have your paycheck in hand, you will feel the exhilaration of having truly EARNED IT. Beta, that is part of 'karma' yoga. 'Karma' means work: the deeds that you perform with passion."

"Papa," I reply. "I am not going on an important job as a doctor, engineer, or a teacher. Come on, I am just going to be making pizzas at the pizza parlor for a few hours during the week."

In a typical teenager fashion, I roll my eyes and say, "Really, it is not a big deal, papa."

My mother, who is in inventory management at the same company my dad works at, has been quiet all this time.

She graduated with a Bachelor's Degree in English Literature in India but never worked outside the home when I was growing up. When our family moved to the United States from India, she decided to enter the work force. She has worked her way up at her job, and as long as I can remember, she has always been happy with every job. She is a genuine hard worker. Her bosses have always loved her.

She now sits down next to me.

"Neeti, there is no work that is more important than another. What is important is how you do something, and not what you do. When you are working at the pizza parlor, put forth your best effort."

"When you are done with your job, come home and be the best student, daughter, sister, and friend that you can be. You have many roles in life, and don't let one role overpower the other. You must have balance in life, but strive to be the best that you can be in each of your roles, no matter what you are doing."

"Bring smiles to your customers," she continues, "and provide such service that the customers will want to come back. It is not about taking an order and carrying the food, drinks and dishes back and forth from the tables on a particular night, but rather it is about making it an experience for you and your customers to remember. Think of all the interesting people you will meet."

"This is your first job, and it is going to create a pathway for you into the future for many other jobs. How you do this job today will either bring the right jobs to you in the future with ease, or you will always fight to find and keep a job that you can be happy at. 'Beta,' which of the two choices do you want in life?"

I remember receiving my first paycheck. It was everything my parents had told me and more. I almost wept when I cashed that check because I knew I had worked hard to earn it.

I was grateful that I had heeded my

parent's words and worked harder than I was required to and accomplished more than my normal job duties of the week. Yes, it felt good. No, it felt GREAT!

Now as I look back over my career as an accountant, I realize how invaluable that one summer evening was with my parents.

This first job experience was a confirmation to me that hard work feels good. Since then, I have gone on to various jobs in my career, always carrying my parent's words close to my heart.

I have taken their advice, added to it, and actually written a prescription for professional and personal success. In this book, I am passing it on to you for your own use.

Don't just read it. Follow it, and don't just follow it for a time. Integrate it into the fabric of your being as a matter of habit.

Here it is:

- Get to work before your start time.

- Be happy and grateful to be there.

- Make a "to do" list every day and every week.

- Don't just make a list. Work your way through the list.

- Read something new daily in your area of expertise.

- Call one person each week in your industry, or area of expertise, just to say, "Hello."

- Attend at least two seminars, continuing education, and networking events every six months.

- While at these events, "work" at "networking" by meeting at least three individuals with whom you can follow up later.

- Keep track of all projects you are working on.

- Give updates to your boss before she has to ask you about the status of a project.

- Subscribe to publications and magazines relevant to your industry.

- Read them.

- Ask yourself the question: "How can I bring value to my company?"

- As you read journals and books, ask yourself if any of the ideas you are reading can apply to your company.

- Collect these ideas and place them in your "Idea Box."

- Don't just sit in your cubicle or office. Walk around and say hello to your colleagues. Get to know them.

- Learn from your colleagues. Ask them questions.

- Keep an updated calendar.

- Be gracious to the employees who

report to you. Acknowledge their accomplishments.

- Never gossip about others. Never.

- Look for other people's strengths and not their weaknesses.

- Have fun at work. I did not say "party" at work. Have "fun" with the "work" that you do. Enjoy it, learn to enjoy it, or move on and find something that you can enjoy.

- Surround yourself with a smart team.

- Delegate with confidence to your team.

- Focus on the important projects first: the projects that will improve the company's bottom line.

- When you make a mistake, admit it and do not make the same mistake again. Chalk up the lessons learned from the mistake to memory, and move on.

- Seek mentors in your field whom you admire and who likewise enjoy mentoring you. Seek their input often.

- Review this list at the end of the week and see how you performed.

BREATHE

BE STILL

SMILE

Directions for use:

Whenever you feel that stress, anger, or frustration is interfering with your ability to function optimally or whenever you begin to feel disconnected, disjointed, and disorganized, take 60 seconds to create your own little mental oasis, and follow three simple steps:

- **Breathe** – With eyes closed, draw in positive energy, and exhale negative energy. (Slow inhalations and slow exhalations, 20 seconds.)

- **Be still** – Go to the center of your being. (Sitting perfectly still, 20 seconds.)

- **Smile** – Turn all negativity, both internal and external, into positive energy. (Eyes still closed, counting silently to 20 in your mind.)

You can follow these steps as often as once an hour or whenever you feel the need for it. This secret EXECUTIVE YOGI technique can help you maximize your performance and your sense of well-being. Regard this as your own secret SIXTY SECOND mental oasis.

CHAPTER FOUR

"The Power Of Action"

CHAPTER FOUR

"The Power Of Action"

Our reputation at work is extremely important. It carries the weight of gold when it is good. As long as I have worked, I have always strived to do my best and contribute as a valued part of the team.

When we are in the office, sometimes it is difficult to concentrate on a project. Most of our days are filled with interruptions: the phone ringing, people stopping by to discuss projects, and even urgent emails.

What can we do?

Here's a little technique I use to carve out a day for myself with minimum interruptions. I probably shouldn't be sharing this because now everyone at my workplace will know about this little trick, and it won't work anymore!

It's very simple:

- I schedule a meeting with myself on my outlook calendar for a couple of hours (or sometimes a whole day) once a week to work on projects.

- Once the calendar is blocked for the meeting, no one else can schedule a meeting with me for that time.

- It allows me time to sit in a conference room or an empty cube away from my office to catch up and work on big projects uninterrupted.

Even if your boss doesn't notice your great work and reward you with a compliment or a raise, you know that you've put in your full share. It will all come back to you. Maybe not today, but when it comes back, it will come back with accumulated interest and dividends. Dividends are sweet, especially when they are unexpected.

I am a teenager. I have been working at an Indian restaurant as a "bus boy," or better put, "bus girl." My job is to clean all the dirty dishes and help with preparation of drinks like "mango lassi" (a blend of mango pulp and yogurt), milk shakes, etc.

The first time I show up for work my manager asks, "Why are you all dressed up in a nice skirt and blouse? As a bus boy, you are allowed to come to work in casual clothes. Shorts, jeans, sweats are all okay."

I smile and nod, but I am recalling my mother's words of wisdom as they have been repeated to me on many occasions:

"When you leave the house, make sure you look clean, polished, and presentable at all times."

I continue to come in dressed-up for my job as bus boy. I load, unload, and re-load the dishwasher with the dirty dishes. I make drinks, and clean everything else I can get my hands on until it shines like the back of my dad's bald head.

Then one Saturday, the busiest day of the week, the headwaiter calls in sick. Guess who is ready to step into that role? Yes — ME!

I am already dressed appropriately, and I know how to handle the customers. It is an opportunity in the making. The owner promotes me from bus boy to waitress the very next day. My salary jumps up overnight!

My mother's advice was right. We should work as hard as we can, put in more than what is required of us, no matter what our title. The right opportunity will then automatically be drawn to us — because we are prepared for it.

I learned another lesson from this experience: When we dress and act like the person we want to become, we turn into that idealized vision of ourselves.

Now that we are focused and committed, thoroughly professional, dedicated to our careers and our organizations, everything always go perfectly, right? — "Wrong!"

Sometimes we hit a bump in the road: challenging people, market corrections, downsizing. Sometimes we even make mistakes. None of us is perfect. Mistakes are a part of life.

But mistakes should not be the end of the story. Mistakes give us an opportunity to learn and grow. They can help strengthen us and make us better.

Let me tell you a story about a mistake I made.

The sun is dazzling as it shines through the office window onto my cubicle, leaving patterns of diamonds dancing off my crystal red bracelet. However, I do not feel the sun's warmth nor do I acknowledge the brightness of the sun. My mind is reeling from an earlier conversation with a co-worker.

I am managing a project related to tax research for the state of Washington, and it has been pointed to me that I have missed one big issue that is important to the client.

My jaw tightens. My lungs feel as if that Indian elephant is sitting on my chest, making it difficult to take a calm breath. I am angry. But, I am not angry at my co-worker. I am angry at myself.

I begin to tick off the role that I played in this mistake:

- I had not reviewed the client information in enough detail.

- I had relied too heavily on the team reporting to me.

- Perhaps the team had needed more guidance from me.

- If I had done a more detailed review, the mistake could have been avoided.

I know that I could come up with a list of legitimate excuses as long as my arm for why the mistake happened.

- I had, in fact, been under the weather that week.

- I had also had out of town guests at home and my daughter was not well either.

- I didn't have enough time to review my team's work because we were under pressure to complete the project in a very short time frame.

But, at the end of the day, I know that these would just be excuses.

As I analyze the causes of the mistake, I realize that given the time pressures and my being under the weather:

- I could have asked a co-worker's assistance in reviewing the work.

- I could have asked for more time from the client.

- I could have been more specific in my expectations of my team.

I spend a lot of time wallowing in my mistake:

> "If only I had read more carefully... if only I had..." On and on...my mind is racing.

And then I realize, "I have to stop this. This is not helping anyone. I must learn from this mistake and vow to never allow something like this to happen again in my career. And, I must apologize. "

I make it a point to remember this incident each and every time I begin working on an important project, and it pushes me to:

- Work twice as hard and concentrate on all the issues.

- Run the facts by someone else who may have a different or better perspective.

- Consult others when I need to.

- Deliver a project that is worth delivering.

We all will make mistakes from time to time. The important thing is to learn from our mistakes and move on. Yes, we may feel like we have lost "face" or let someone down. That can be a good thing, if we use that feeling to propel us to do better next time.

BREATHE

BE STILL

SMILE

Directions for use:

Whenever you feel that stress, anger, or frustration is interfering with your ability to function optimally or whenever you begin to feel disconnected, disjointed, and disorganized, take 60 seconds to create your own little mental oasis, and follow three simple steps:

- **Breathe** – With eyes closed, draw in positive energy, and exhale negative energy. (Slow inhalations and slow exhalations, 20 seconds.)

- **Be still** – Go to the center of your being. (Sitting perfectly still, 20 seconds.)

- **Smile** – Turn all negativity, both internal and external, into positive energy. (Eyes still closed, counting silently to 20 in your mind.)

You can follow these steps as often as once an hour or whenever you feel the need for it. This secret EXECUTIVE YOGI technique can help you maximize your performance and your sense of well-being. Regard this as your own secret SIXTY SECOND mental oasis.

CHAPTER FIVE

"The Power Of The Body"

CHAPTER FIVE

"The Power Of The Body"

Yogis take care of their physical bodies. They understand that their bodies are necessary vehicles through which they can experience life. Yogis know that they can reach their goals more easily if their bodies and minds are aligned in good health.

We all understand that we should take care of our bodies. Many of us take up some kind of fitness program. We join a gym, buy expensive equipment, start walking or even biking to work.

What about you? Have you ever paid for membership to a health club, or bought exercise equipment?

Maybe you followed an exercise regimen for a little while, and then you lost interest.

Have you ever felt pumped up one day and signed up for a dance or yoga class?

Maybe you went to a few classes and then became busy with work, family, or social obligations, and stopped going.

If this is true for you, don't feel bad. It's true for most people.

Over time, most of us stop going to the gym. We stop using our fancy new fitness equipment. We tell ourselves that we are too busy to find the time to walk or bike.

Our excuses are legion:

• Working out is time consuming.

• It is boring.

• The gym is too far away.

• We are too tired after work to go to the gym.

• We don't have time to shower during our lunch break and get back to work on time.

• It is easier and more fun to read a book, watch a video, or go out to eat.

Fitness becomes a chore rather than a fun part of life.

So what can we do?

- First of all, we should not set goals that are unachievable.

- Second, we should not make a big deal out of it. Fifteen minutes is better than zero minutes.

- Third, if we find we aren't enjoying what we are doing, we can try something else.

What we do for exercise is not important. What is important is that we find something we enjoy enough that we will follow through. If we are bored with running on the treadmill, we can take classes in judo, modern dance, or swimming. Find out what you enjoy.

Fitness was not an issue when I was a young girl growing up in India. We never had to think about fitness. I don't think we even had a gym or fitness club in the whole town. No one owned a workout machine or had a set of weights at home. But that didn't mean we were not fit.

Everyday, I could not wait to get off the school bus, rush through supper, and run off to meet my neighborhood playmates. We would go from house-to-house collecting the whole crowd, one-by-one, until we had a bustling team of five to ten children. Both boys and girls played together.

We would play cricket until it was dark. No one moved from the fields until we would hear our mothers, shouting from the front verandas for us to return home for dinner.

Grudgingly, we would throw the bats down, count up the scores, and vow to return the next day to beat the other team. We managed to get our exercise as we played and we had fun.

There were other days when we'd rather go pick mangoes or guavas from a neighbor's yard. Panting and pink-cheeked, we would scramble up into the trees, swinging from limb to limb, caught up in the exhilaration of finding the juicy fruit.

"Plunk!" — "Plunk!" — Plunk!"

The fruit would land on the ground and we would rush down, gathering our skirts and shirts together to hold and hide our precious loot. Often, the yard owner would notice us, and chase after us with a stick threatening to tell our parents.

The yard owners or the "malis" (gardeners), who tended to the fruit gardens, never complained to our parents. But, I think they enjoyed scaring us and running after us, until we were screaming at the top of our lungs and running helter-skelter in all directions. Later, we would gather on the roof of my house to count our loot and devour the fruits of our hard work.

As usual, we would sit around until it was dark and then our mothers would start shouting out our names to return home for dinner. They often wondered why we didn't have much of an appetite for dinner, or why we often complained of a tummy ache.

After the dinner dishes were put away, my parents, little brother, and I would hit the town for an after-dinner walk. Were my parents going on these walks to burn calories? I think not, or at least consciously. I think the real reason my parents took us for a walk was so they could meet up with their friends.

Our parents would connect with their buddies, and their buddies' buddies, give hugs to each other, shake hands, or greet each other with a "namaste" (I honor you). I vividly remember these family after-dinner walks in the evenings.

We would walk around and around the block, talking about our day and planning the next day. My brother and I were always ahead of mom and dad, egging each other on to see who was the fastest runner. We were having fun and getting our exercise.

"Let's run up to the corner market down the block," my brother would say.

I, being the older one, usually came in ahead of my brother. But, there were times when I would let him beat me. He would proudly reach the finish line, which was the corner market, so tiny it could not have been larger than two feet wide and two feet long.

Papa would buy us each candy or peanuts from the corner store. It was his way of rewarding the winner of the race — but being a soft touch, he usually bought the little treats for both of us.

"You both won," he would say. "We are part of one family, and in life, if any one member wins, then it is really a victory for all of us to celebrate."

As my brother and I munched on our peanuts or candy, other children, with their families, would join us. Then the races would start again among us children, while the parents walked together discussing the latest Bollywood movies, planning the next card game, or a potluck.

After a half an hour of this routine, I would be tired and come back to my dad begging him to carry me the rest of the way home on his shoulders. Instead, he would walk us to the next bus stop, and we would sit down on the bench and rest.

But how long can a child sit down?

Within a few minutes, I would pull on my dad's sleeve and ask him to lift me up high enough so that I could grab hold of the top of the poles that held the little bus-stop shelter in place. I would then slither down the pole in glee.

"Put me up there again papa," I would say.

My baby brother would follow the same routine on the other side of the bus stop. So, my dad would walk back and forth between the two poles, lifting my brother and then me, up to the top of the poles which seemed as high as the peaks of Mount Everest to us then. He didn't need to lift weights. He lifted children for exercise — literally and in turn lifted our soaring little spirits.

Those childhood memories of fun evenings with my family left their mark on me. Now I have my own children, and we love to go for long walks together. We get our exercise and spend time talking to each other without the distractions of the phone ringing or the television blaring.

Sometimes we take a few judo lessons or swim lessons together. I no longer play cricket or field hockey like I did in my childhood, but I enjoy playing basketball, soccer, or tennis with my family. I am terrible at all of these games. But that doesn't matter. What matters is that we are all staying active, exercising our muscles and our lungs.

As you exercise, throw your mind and body fully into the routine. Actively think of the muscles you are using and visualize them getting stronger. "Intend" your body to feel better and vital. Realize that as you exercise your outer body and muscles, you are also exercising the internal organs and making them strong.

Fresh air is very important for our lungs. Open the windows in your house to bring in the fresh air. Take a few deep breaths. Let the lungs expand and contract. This simple exercise of inhaling and exhaling helps exercise your internal organs. It gets them fresh oxygen.

My favorite forms of exercise are yoga and dance. I start my day with a yoga routine called "suryah namaskar" (salute to the sun pose).

At the end of the day, I slip into bed and finish the day with more yoga basics. "Why in bed?" you may ask.

The answer to that question is that it works for me. I know myself. I would not spend time on the floor doing a yoga routine at the end of the day.

However, once I am in bed, yoga helps me relax and fall asleep. I do not view it as exercise. That is why I have been able to maintain the yoga routine for many years.

Traditionally, Yogis in India practiced the art of yoga, and it has become very popular now throughout the world. It can be either a rigorous, or a gentle form of exercise, depending upon the needs of each individual.

I like yoga because it not only tones the body, it also exercises the mind. Yoga is a discipline.

After my morning meditation, I stay on the yoga mat for a little longer, and practice yoga poses. I learned yoga at the age of thirteen as I watched my mother take lessons in our house.

My mother and her yoga instructor would practice the art of yoga, stretching in every direction on the floor of our living room. I was fascinated. I copied their steps and since then have continued to practice basic yoga "asanas" (positions).

You don't have to be flexible and in excellent physical shape to do yoga. You can practice yoga no matter what shape you are in today. All you need is a yoga mat and comfortable clothes.

Begin by taking classes at your local yoga studio or pick up a yoga video.

Yoga has many benefits. It teaches you to concentrate as you hold your body in a yoga position without faltering and falling down. You begin to gain physical strength as your muscles get used to yoga.

Besides strength, your body feels fluid and flexible. You begin to feel more comfortable within your body. It gives you a better posture so that when you walk, you have an air of confidence, strength, and grace.

I have found that yoga and meditation are closely tied to each other. Just as meditation focuses on your breath to calm and sharpen the mind, yoga focuses on your breath and poses to strengthen and flex your body.

You don't have to do a headstand or a back bend like a yogi can, but you can most certainly lie down and begin with the basic poses that allow you to stretch your body and eventually your mind.

Find an exercise routine that you enjoy, and no matter how tired you are or whatever mood you are in, follow through with your routine. Visualize the beautiful body you'll have. Let that be your motivation.

If you're tired, you don't have to do the fifty sit-ups that you might normally do on a good day. You can do five instead. It is easy to convince your mind to do five. Five is far better than none. The trick is to do a little everyday.

If you have had an especially challenging day, have been traveling, or working extra hours, and you could not make time for exercise, do not make a big deal of it. Just start again the next day. Or the next week. Just don't give up on exercising.

If you have no time for classes, take your workout shoes with you to work. Go for a brisk walk at lunch or break time. Take the stairs to get to your office. Run up and down the stairs in the middle of the day.

Take a walk with your family in the evenings. Play ball with your children. Shoot hoops. Hit balls on the green. Golf. Do something. The benefit comes from exercising a little every day.

I have made it simple. I have made it fun. Go find a simple routine and incorporate it in your daily life.

BREATHE

BE STILL

SMILE

Directions for use:

Whenever you feel that stress, anger, or frustration is interfering with your ability to function optimally or whenever you begin to feel disconnected, disjointed, and disorganized, take 60 seconds to create your own little mental oasis, and follow three simple steps:

- **Breathe** – With eyes closed, draw in positive energy, and exhale negative energy. (Slow inhalations and slow exhalations, 20 seconds.)

- **Be still** – Go to the center of your being. (Sitting perfectly still, 20 seconds.)

- **Smile** – Turn all negativity, both internal and external, into positive energy. (Eyes still closed, counting silently to 20 in your mind.)

You can follow these steps as often as once an hour or whenever you feel the need for it. This secret EXECUTIVE YOGI technique can help you maximize your performance and your sense of well-being. Regard this as your own secret SIXTY SECOND mental oasis.

CHAPTER SIX

"The Power Of Food"

CHAPTER SIX

"The Power Of Food"

Agra, India:

I am a child of eight, sitting on the balcony of the old hospital where I have come with my family to welcome a new-born cousin. The hospital is surrounded by tall trees that have monkeys hanging from their branches.

I am eating a papaya, while I watch a burly monkey sitting on the branch of a tree above. His face is as dark as the darkest night, and his pink nostrils flare wide as his sharp red eyes lock onto mine.

I bite into the plump fruit. Bright yellow juice runs down my chin, and then, the monkey, faster than lightening it seems to me, leaps from the tree, snatches the papaya right out of my hand, and flees back up into the treetop.

I begin to wail — partly because I am scared to death, but mainly because the monkey has stolen my papaya. My grandmother comes running out of the hospital room and tries to soothe me as I continue to wail.

I clutch tightly to her sari and sob, while shaking my small fist at the monkey, and demanding that he bring my papaya back.

It isn't that I am really hungry. It's just that I want to eat that papaya!

Food is the fuel that provides us energy and keeps us going. If we let the fuel tank run dry, we become lethargic and weak. We may even get sick. The right quantity of nutritious food is essential for the well-being of our bodies and minds.

How often do we refuel our body's fuel tank before it is even half-empty?

We see a commercial on television for sizzling shrimp fajitas or crunchy potato chips and our mouth starts to water. All we can think about is how fast we can put that food into our mouths.

Rather than relying on internal indicators like hunger pangs or a drop in energy, we respond to external factors like TV commercials or the ubiquitous aromas that seem to permeate every public space. The aroma hits us, we salivate, and hungry or not, we want food now!

I was fifteen years old when my family and I moved from India to Los Angeles. One of the very first things that struck me was the enormous size of grocery stores. They were bigger than the cricket fields in my little hometown of Ranchi.

I was used to eating either oatmeal or corn flakes for breakfast, and for variety, my mother used to sprinkle brown sugar, jam, or extra cream on the cereal.

I walked into a grocery store in Los Angeles for the first time with my aunt, and there were endless rows of cereal boxes, lined up like a long winding snake. Every color, shape, and size I could imagine. I was most fascinated by Trix cereal, which had multi-colored pieces of cereal in it. I could not wait to wake up every morning to enjoy a large bowl of Trix. The week after that, it was Apple Jacks. And the week after that, it was another bright box that happened to catch my fancy.

We live in a country where food for most of us is not only abundant, it is too abundant. We have only to look around us to see the results. Many adults, and even children, are so overweight that their health is at risk and their lives in jeopardy.

So what can we do?

First and foremost, we can set limits on what we will and will not put into our mouths. When we are tempted, we can taste something, savor it, and enjoy the sweet, salty, or pungent taste without eating the whole thing.

Remember that the first spoonful or the first bite tastes the best. We can take a bite or two. We can tell ourselves how good the food tastes. Then, we can put it down. Then, we can tell ourselves how good we feel about not eating the whole thing. We can remind ourselves that we are on our way to feeling better and living healthier.

Three of my favorite treats are tres-leche cake, crème bruele, and flan. Anytime I am tempted to indulge in any of these desserts, I conjure up two pictures in my head side by side:

One picture is of me looking beautiful and in good health, the other one of me looking fat and lethargic.

I focus on the beautiful picture for a few seconds, and when I turn my focus back to the table, I am no longer interested in the so called "bad foods." Try it. It works.

We need to pay attention to our bodies when we eat. Before eating or drinking anything, we should stop for a second and ask ourselves if we really want to indulge in it.

Will it enhance the healthy picture we have of ourselves in our heads, or will it pull us toward the fat and lethargic picture? Then, we can make our decision. Whenever we eat, we are making a choice.

Moderation is really the key. There are occasions when we can choose to fully enjoy a calorie-laden meal, followed by dessert, and then a cappuccino. But, the trick is to limit these meals to only a few times a month. We don't want to let this kind of eating become an everyday habit.

Fresh fruits like apples are easy to take with us, and can be substituted for high calorie fried foods.

I personally have a rule to never finish everything on my plate. (Yes, I know that this runs counter to what most of our parents taught us growing up.) Rebel against this notion and leave a few calories on the plate.

I also eat several small meals during the day. That way, I pace myself and do not overeat by having a large meal in one sitting. I get used to eating smaller portions, and pretty soon it becomes a habit.

As I sit down to eat, I make a point to enjoy every bite. As I eat, I tell myself that I am gaining energy from the foods to help boost my energy, give me strength, and fuel for life.

My grandfather, whom I lovingly call "bowji" meaning "the wise grandpa," is asking me to stop eating and listen to him.

"Neeta," he says, using his nickname for me instead of Neeti, my real name. "All food that you eat has 'pran' (life forces) within it. The purpose of eating is to transfer that 'pran' into yourself, so you will have vitality."

I listen to him, and then continue to wolf down the food, until he stops me again.

With a tender hand on my wrist, he looks into my eyes and says, "What's the hurry,

'Beta' (daughter)? The food is not going anywhere. Chew your food slowly, think about every bite you take as to how it is helping your body, feel the saliva build up as you think of the food you are about to eat, have a bite, and then put your fork down and feel the satisfaction of the meal. Then you can start again..."

I am a grown woman now, and my beloved "bowji" is no longer here, but his words play in my head every time I sit down for a meal. I don't have to eat as much to gain satisfaction because I see food as a source of energy. Food is the fuel that keeps me going like the energizer bunny. The "pran" keeps pulsating in me throughout the day.

As children, we all learned in our science class that our body is made up mostly of water. We must continually replenish it.

I have a beautiful china cup on my desk and keep it filled with hot water, herbal tea, regular water, or ice cubes depending upon the weather and my mood that day. I enjoy sipping from my cup not just because of the contents, but because the beautiful flowers that adorn the outside of the cup make it a lovely experience. Drinking from that cup gives me a feeling of elegance that encourages me to stay hydrated.

While eating in moderation and drinking plenty of water contribute to the well-being of our bodies, vitamins and minerals can also be beneficial. (Be sure to consult with your doctor to determine what supplements may work best for you based on your age and lifestyle.)

Sometimes small changes can have big results. A few years back I stopped putting sugar into my tea. My idea was to avoid those few extra calories, and also to limit my intake of processed sugars, which are bad for the body.

One week passed, and I still craved the sugar. Two weeks passed, and I still wanted that sweetness in my tea.

Would I make it, or would I succumb to my sweet tooth? I wasn't sure.

Then I recalled what my dad had said to me almost ten years ago.

Torrance Memorial Hospital, Torrance, California, (just outside Los Angeles):

Papa is lying in the hospital, suffering from a heart attack. He is writhing in pain. His forehead is wrinkled, and his sharp eyes are clouded with fear. My mom, little brother, aunt, uncle, and four couples (my parents' closest friends), are all here at the hospital.

Doctors are buzzing around Papa.

He looks at me, and begins to rattle off instructions: the location where he stores his life insurance policy and bank account documents.

"We won't need them, Papa," I say. "You are going to be fine."

He ignores me and continues to give me instructions. His face changes colors — going from "samosa brown" to that of "blood-red" tandoori chicken.

Then he is wheeled away. I feel a dull numbness around my heart.

We wait. It's a long and restless wait.

Finally, Papa is wheeled back into the room.

My little brother grabs Papa's hand, as though he can hold Papa here with us in this world. I am weak from the stress. I can only imagine what my exhausted mother is feeling as she looks at her husband and best friend lying in the hospital bed.

Papa looks up at us and speaks:

"This is my fault. I should have listened to all of you when you urged me to stop smoking years ago. You should not have to go through feeling the fear of losing me. Besides, I want to be around to see you children get married and have your kids. I promise to give up smoking right this minute, cold turkey!"

Papa stuck to his words. I knew it was very, very hard for him the first week. It was even tougher the second week, and even more trying the third week. But by the time the fourth week rolled around, it was starting to get easier for him. He tells us that after a month it became a habit not to smoke.

I remembered this as I struggled to keep from putting sugar into my tea. Guess what? After the fourth week, I was thoroughly enjoying every sip of my steaming hot "chai" without the sugar. In fact, I didn't even notice it. As a matter of fact, not long after that when I was visiting a friend, who added sugar to my tea, I didn't even enjoy the taste.

This small example shows just how adaptable our bodies and minds are to any new habit, good or bad. Habits (good or bad) are hard to break, but if we hang in there (a month is about all the time it takes to break a habit), and consciously think about the positive change we are making, we can do it.

When we are busy, we may tend to eat on the run. We may go through a fast food drive-in. We may even convince ourselves that we are too busy doing "important things" and can't spare time to eat a proper meal.

The best way to counteract this excuse is to sit down and make a menu with our families at the beginning of each week. We can also buy healthy snacks, fruits, and salads to take with us to work.

By planning ahead, we can munch throughout the day on good snacks.

At lunch time, go enjoy a light healthy lunch, or sit back at your desk and take pleasure in the meal.

Yogis are disciplined when it comes to food. They consume only what is necessary for the body to survive and to provide strength. They savor food and enjoy it as a gift.

You can gain the same discipline with food. Focus on your intake. Eat in moderation. Savor it. Enjoy it. Nourish yourself. Be healthy.

BREATHE

BE STILL

SMILE

Directions for use:

Whenever you feel that stress, anger, or frustration is interfering with your ability to function optimally or whenever you begin to feel disconnected, disjointed, and disorganized, take 60 seconds to create your own little mental oasis, and follow three simple steps:

- Breathe – With eyes closed, draw in positive energy, and exhale negative energy. (Slow inhalations and slow exhalations, 20 seconds.)

- Be still – Go to the center of your being. (Sitting perfectly still, 20 seconds.)

- Smile – Turn all negativity, both internal and external, into positive energy. (Eyes still closed, counting silently to 20 in your mind.)

You can follow these steps as often as once an hour or whenever you feel the need for it. This secret EXECUTIVE YOGI technique can help you maximize your performance and your sense of well-being. Regard this as your own secret SIXTY SECOND mental oasis.

CHAPTER SEVEN

"The Power Of Image"

CHAPTER SEVEN

"The Power Of Image"

Town of Ranchi, India — The Dewan Family House:

Rain is beating down on the roof and the wind is tugging on the trees in the garden. The hail smacking against the window of my bedroom sounds like a child hitting balls with a cricket bat.

I am tucked away inside my house. I look out at the rainstorm. Boredom simmers in my big dark brown eyes. I twirl my fingers around my hair, staring into the wet world outside — a place where I am not allowed to go.

"You can't go out," my mother had said. "You could catch a cold."

Before I could open my mouth to argue, she'd continued, "And yes, I don't care if other children are allowed to stay outside in the rain!"

That settled it. I am stuck inside. Doing nothing. Feeling very sorry for myself.

Then, my eyes fall on the old trunk in the corner. It is silver in color, shining brightly with mysteries locked within.

I peek my head out of my bedroom door. I can hear my mother talking to a neighbor from the kitchen window.

None of us had telephones then. The windows of the two houses face each other, and my mother and the "auntie" (we addressed all our parent's friends and neighbors as aunties and uncles) next door are sharing a day's worth of happenings through the windows.

My mother has thrown open the window and called out our neighbor's name. Our neighbor has appeared at the other end of the window, and they are talking as though they are connected by an invisible telephone line.

Their conversation is being broadcast loudly for anyone in the neighborhood to hear. Other "mommies" and "aunties" are flinging their windows open, and joining this "Chat Room."

With my mother hosting the chat room, the coast is clear. No one is looking.

Stealthily, with my eyes shining and my little hands shaking, I try to pull open the clasp on the "mystical" trunk. The clasp is stuck.

The trunk is almost as tall as I am. I climb up on it, and sitting on top, I try to pry the lock open. It groans a little.

By now, my heart is thumping with excitement. With a loud groan, the trunk finally flies open, as if it is a monster that is going to swallow me whole.

I grab a flashlight and carefully climb into the trunk so I can explore its contents. I land on something soft and silky.

My flashlight reveals a mosaic of bright fabrics in every color imaginable. I clutch at the items and manage to pull some of them out of the trunk.

I close the bedroom door and flip the fluorescent light switch on. The light flickers a few times before it steadies itself into a brilliant blaze.

I squeal with delight as my eyes feast on the silken treasures that envelope me. They are my mother's old saris (5 feet of cloth that wraps around to make an elegant gown), as well as scarves and shawls.

I am especially drawn to a hot flamingo pink sari. It has gold threads running wild across its length in shapes of leaves, flowers, and birds. I wrap it around me and walk back and forth, prancing like a princess.

That day, I fell in love with the sight of beautiful fabrics, their silken feel on the skin, and the vibrant colors that wake up the senses. Ever since that day, I never let bad weather become an opportunity for bore-dom.

When storms blew in, I would spend hours playing dress-up, pretending to be Queen Mumtaz in whose honor King Shah Jahan built the magnificent memorial to love called the "Taj Mahal." (I was, after all, born in the same city where the Taj Mahal stands: the City of Agra, India.)

It's not just little girls in India who think about their appearance.

In our Western world, both men and women often fret over their appearance.

Thoughts like these may swim through our heads:

- Am I too fat?

- Am I too short?

- I don't have enough hair!

- Does she find me attractive?

- Does my stomach stick out too much?

- Do I have thunder thighs?

- My nose is too big!

- If only my legs were a little longer.

- I am too skinny...I wish I had more curves.

Do any of these sound familiar to you?

I think we all have thoughts similar to these from time to time. The only thing to do is to take control of them and chuck them right out the window. None of us was born with the perfect body or the perfect look.

We must eliminate the word "perfection" from our vocabulary.

We must accept who we are, our varied shapes and sizes, our different hair and skin colors, and all the physical attributes that are beyond our control.

Once we come to terms with who we are, we can then begin to enjoy the things that are indeed within our power to control.

Do you remember a special occasion when you dressed up and felt really good? Recall that feeling vividly. Harness it. There is nothing stopping you from feeling that way right now. Today.

The warm smile that you flash to a neighbor, the sparkle in your eyes, the joy in your heart, or the spring in your step when you do things you enjoy, convey the grace, elegance, and character that lie within you. This is true beauty.

Some of us may have the means to splurge on our wardrobe and personal treatments, while others of us struggle to buy that one business suit. It doesn't matter which category we fall into. There are simple ways of creating our own style and taking care of our appearance.

When it comes to wardrobe, we can start with the basic pieces: a couple of navy and black slacks (and/or skirts for the ladies), solid dark-colored blazers, several white shirts, and two pairs of nice dress shoes for men and pumps or flats for women.

Professional dress styles, customs, and dress codes vary from company to company, city to city, country to country, and even from one continent to another continent.

What is acceptable in one setting may not be acceptable in another. We need to keep our eyes open and observe how people dress in our organization and city.

For a job interview, or a meeting with people we haven't met in person before, it is best if we dress conservatively. A dark suit with a white shirt is a safe bet for the first meeting. Our clothing should exude an aura of confidence and conservatism. We do not want our clothes to overpower the interview. Rather, our clothes should compliment the interview process.

Several corporations now allow business casual attire, whereas others continue to follow the traditional conservative blue or black suit dress code for work. We need to know what the rules are, both formal and informal.

How are others in our organization dressed? Dress to blend in. Strive to be one of the best dressed but not "The Best Dressed," unless you are the CEO or president. Accessories such as a nice watch, a leather belt, a pin, or a scarf can help complete the professional look.

We should invest in a few good pairs of leather shoes and maintain them. Scuffed shoes have no place in the workplace. Our shoes should be polished and buffed at all times. It shows that we pay attention to details.

If we work in a business casual environment, we should keep a spare blazer (and tie for men) in our office or car. We never know when we may be called upon to meet with top management or a client. At a moment's notice, we should be ready to transform in SIXTY SECONDS into a polished business person, who is presentable, and one who can host a last-minute meeting with ease.

Just as we dress according to the dress code at our workplace, we should do the same when meeting a client. If possible, we should do some upfront research to find out the dress code of people we are meeting with. If they are from a casual workforce, we don't want to show up to a meeting with them in a three piece suit. It may make them uncomfortable. By the same token, if our client has a business dress code, we should not wear khakis and a polo shirt when we meet with them.

I'm sure we've all worked with someone who is a hard worker, but shows up to work in somewhat rumpled shirts, threads hanging off his or her twenty year old slacks, ring around the collar or cuffs, or a haircut that is the artistic creation of his or her spouse?

This does not project the right image for a professional. When we are hired as a professional, it is expected that we will invest some of our paycheck in clean and decent clothes and grooming. This investment is not only in our wardrobe, but is truly an investment in our career.

The outward image we project is what others see first. Secondly, they see the quality of our work. It makes sense to ensure that the quality of our wardrobe and grooming should be up to par with the quality of our work.

Many businesses today that follow a business-casual dress code are facing problems with employees who interpret the code too liberally. This newly acquired freedom from business suits and ties can be dangerous to our careers if we are not careful.

The original idea behind business-casual was to help employees feel comfortable as they worked. Employers and clients still expect their employees and consultants to be professional in their appearance when transacting business. Hawaiian and vendor logo shirts are best left for the weekend.

Some major "no-no's" for work are showing the tummy and cleavage. One of the worst offenses I see is women wearing short shirts that pull up to show their stomachs when they raise their hands, paired with the new style of a hip-hugging pants that pull down when they bend to pick up a file.

Tank tops, sweats, blue jeans (unless there's a specially designated jean day), flip flops, and visible large tattoos are not business attire, or even close to the definition of business-casual attire, and should be strictly reserved for our weekends and evenings.

Men and women in most business sectors should refrain from body piercing.

Jewelry in good taste is okay for work, as long as it does not get in the way of work or make noise that is distracting to others. It goes without saying that besides proper business attire, we must maintain impeccable hygiene.

In today's global world, people often move from one city to the next or even to an entirely different continent to pursue business and career opportunities.

As the saying goes, "When in Rome, do as the Romans do." We should dress appropriately for the area of the world we are in. What is our environment like? What are the people wearing? What is acceptable and what is not?

These are the questions we should be asking ourselves as we observe the global workforce. This conscious review will help us acclimate ourselves fast, and provide us with an advantage to boost our work performance.

Directions for use:

Whenever you feel that stress, anger, or frustration is interfering with your ability to function optimally or whenever you begin to feel disconnected, disjointed, and disorganized, take 60 seconds to create your own little mental oasis, and follow three simple steps:

- **Breathe** – With eyes closed, draw in positive energy, and exhale negative energy. (Slow inhalations and slow exhalations, 20 seconds.)

- **Be still** – Go to the center of your being. (Sitting perfectly still, 20 seconds.)

- **Smile** – Turn all negativity, both internal and external, into positive energy. (Eyes still closed, counting silently to 20 in your mind.)

You can follow these steps as often as once an hour or whenever you feel the need for it. This secret EXECUTIVE YOGI technique can help you maximize your performance and your sense of well-being. Regard this as your own secret SIXTY SECOND mental oasis.

CHAPTER EIGHT

"The Power Of Fun"

CHAPTER EIGHT

"The Power Of Fun"

Ambala, Northern India, The huge
mansion of "Nana" (Grandpa) and "Nani"
(Grandma) where cousins come from all
over India to spend time during the summer:

The verandah at my grandparents' house
has short white pillars outlining its perim-
eter. Along the inside wall are doors leading
to different rooms of the house.

On the right side of the verandah hangs
a swing. The swing is my solace on long
and lazy summer afternoons.

Today, I am roller skating on the verandah, and as I pick up speed, I grab hold of
the swing and pull myself around. I am being careful because many times in the past, I
have lost my balance and hit the floor hard.

Whenever I fall, my little brother squeals
with laughter, but he is also the first one to

help me up when I fall.

Sometimes when I fall, I pretend that I have fainted. I lie there without making a sound. My little brother rushes over to me. He puts his pudgy little arms around me, and tries to shake me out of it.

Very slowly, I open my eyes, and his face bursts into a smile.

Sometimes my brother and I fight because I get upset with him for trying to follow me everywhere I go. But he follows me anyway. I am his big "didi" (sister).

On the verandah, two fans constantly buzz overhead, feebly trying to dispel the heat. Even the slight breeze is hot. My little body is enveloped by the sweltering Indian heat. There is no escape.

Then my grandmother comes out. Her gray-and-black hair is pulled back into a little bun, and she has a gold bracelet around her tiny wrist.

She is holding a tray full of tall cold glasses of "Nimbu Sherbet" (homemade lemonade) for my cousins, my brother, and me in one hand. Her other hand grips the walking stick she must use to walk.

We all run to Grandma and we gulp the lemonade down. She watches us with wide loving eyes.

Beyond the verandah is a wide grassy front lawn. Exotic velvet-like brightly-colored flowers are planted in the middle, there's a vegetable garden to the right and there is green foliage surrounding the garden. The noise from the gardener watering the plants echoes all around us.

Grandpa is out in the yard, waving yet to another friend or acquaintance of his, and asking them to join him in the garden for tea.

Grandma sees the guests arriving, and begins giving instructions to the house servant to run and buy "jalebis," (a bright orange Indian dessert that is filled with nothing but heavenly sugar).

I am happy. I do a dance on the wet grass in my bare feet. The grass tingles, and mud leaves its artwork on my feet. As my grandfather's guests continue to appear and disappear throughout the afternoon, I feast on the "sweet things." It is a wonderful childhood.

"It is 'Oh, so good!'" I tell myself.

It is early evening, and the air begins to cool down. Grandma and Grandpa, as part of their daily evening ritual, are leaving for the Ambala Club House. They will spend a few hours there amongst the warmth of friends, sometimes talking, sometimes walking. Maybe they will also play bridge or rummy.

In the meantime, their children (my parents and uncles and aunts) are gathering on the flat rooftop of the house to set up beds for the night. It is too hot to sleep indoors. They are placing comforters on the portable beds on the roof, and filling clay pots with drinking water for the night.

After dinner, we will lie on our backs, looking up at the clear sky while we count the stars, tell jokes and sing Bollywood songs.

Now, I am the mother. It is another parching hot day in Southern California, and the light wind is slapping my face.

"Mom, this is the best day of my life," my son shouts to me as he takes yet another jump into the cool waters of the pool.

This is not the first time I have heard him say this. It has become a habit for him. And, it has become a habit for my husband and me to create many more days like this one when my son continues to repeat the words: "This is the best day of my life."

Perhaps, it was the loving family I grew up with, or the relaxed atmosphere of summers in Northern India. Perhaps, it was the good food, fun, and laughter that surrounded me, but I cannot remember more relaxed and happier times than those wonderful summers.

When I look back at my wonderful childhood days filled with fun, family, friends, and laughter, I want my own son and daughter to one day look back at their lives, with the same sense of nostalgia. Then, I want them to carry the legacy into the future, and create the same memories for their children.

I know that we all get busy at work, and that we are also busy at home with all the tasks necessary to maintain our households in good order. However, no matter how much we have to do, we must not allow ourselves to be so busy that we forget to treat ourselves to the gift of friends and family.

We must take the time to weave the fabric of love and friendships into our lives. In the long run, these are the relationships that will matter the most to us. They will fill our lives with purpose, and warm our hearts and souls.

My husband, children, and I have crafted a Family Mission Statement. It hangs on the refrigerator where we can see it daily. Its message is imprinted in our daily activities.

The underlying message of our Family Mission Statement is to encourage each other to be the best that we can be as individuals and as a family. To grow, to learn, to live fully, love deeply, and laugh heartily. If any one of us strays from this message, (after all, we all have bad days), we remind each other to look at the statement and get back into the right frame of mind before too much time has elapsed.

Another simple technique is to journal together. Before the start of the week, my husband and I often sit down together and plan the week. We touch on each category of life that is important to us: family, friends, finances, and so on.

We take SIXTY SECONDS to jot down what we will do for each category that week. The children often join us and share their ideas. As the week goes by, we review the journal to see how we are progressing. At the end of the week, we sit down and review our weekly plan to determine if we accomplished the goals. We put a big smiley face next to the categories we did well in, and a frowning face on the ones we need to put more effort in.

We acknowledge the efforts of each family member and give a figurative "kick in the behind" to a family member if it is justified. This simple exercise takes very little time, but it provides direction to our busy lives.

It helps us to focus not only on our work, but on other things that matter as well. We use scrapbooks and albums to serve as memory joggers of the good times.

What types of memories are you creating for yourself and your family? Why not begin to carry a camera with you whenever possible, especially when you are out with friends and family?

Capture the smiles, tears of joy, the picnics, the vacations, family dinners, performances, and celebrations. Make it a point to get the pictures developed by the following weekend. Then, put them in an album. You may even consider adding captions to these pictures as you recall the feelings that are captured in them.

From time to time, take these albums out and recall the good times you had with those special friends and family members. I personally love to look at albums because the memories come rushing back.

The past good times merge into the present, and it takes me right back to the time when:

- My children were born.

- My daughter found the bright pink shell in the ocean.

- My son looked at a sculpture with an intrigued look at an art festival.

- My mother-in-law hugged me tightly as I was leaving for a business trip, and showered me with her blessings.

- My husband suddenly bent down to kiss me on the beach.

- My brother and I danced together to a new song.

- My parents retired and were leaving Los Angeles to go back to India to live and how we hugged. (When I look at the photo of us saying, "Good-bye," I can almost taste the salty tears that ran down my cheeks.)

Memories are important. They keep us connected in a special way to events, places, and people. Albums and scrapbooks create a visual history of our lives which we can pass on to future generations to come.

Our minds are wonderful and complex. They can be conditioned to think in certain ways: negatively or positively. We have the choice. We can empower ourselves when we think positively, and focus our minds on:

- Good times in life.

- People who uplift us rather than tear us down.

- Activities which invigorate us rather than depress us.

We should maintain our ties to friends and colleagues. Here's a simple way that I stay in touch. I maintain an updated business Rolodex and personal address book that has the phone numbers and email addresses of my circle of friends and colleagues.

I go through this list once every three months, and place a call or send an email to the people who:

- Matter to me.

- With whom I want to create better relationships.

- Those who may need a loving phone call from me.

All it takes is SIXTY SECONDS to run down this list.

I am also a big believer in vacations. It is even better when I can enjoy these vacations with friends and family. I am blessed to have a husband who feels the same way and takes charge of planning vacations for the family throughout the year.

If we cannot get away for a week to ten days at a time due to job constrains or other obligations, we can go away for a weekend. We often drive to a nearby resort. We make sure to fill these weekend retreats with unstructured leisure-time, a good book, or whatever activities that make our family happy.

We always come back feeling invigorated, and more importantly, we know that we have actively created good times we can use to focus our minds — memories that we can use to train our brains to feel happy.

Once we get back to the normal work week busy mode, our brain jumpstarts as if it has been given new batteries. Our productivity at work and school soars.

For some of us, money constraints can be a roadblock to planning vacations or weekend getaways. However, many things in life are free or inexpensive. We can take a trip to the local park, zoo, beach, library, a free summer park concert series sponsored by our city, a day in our own backyard, or at the community swimming pool.

Woodland Hills, California:

What a sight it is! We are at our neighborhood park sitting on a blanket spread over the grass as my son shoots hoops and my daughter plays on the monkey bars. We notice a family to our right enjoying a truly joyful day in the park.

They have set up a large tent with a small table inside it where their toddler child plays with his crayons, another table that is piled up with food, a large cooler filled with drinks, and two lounge chairs. The wife is sprawled out on a chair reading a novel. The husband has the radio tuned to a sporting event and is enjoying the play-by-play commentary.

What strikes me most is the fact that they have transformed the park into their own little "vacation sanctuary." This family is having a great time in the park. It does not matter to them that they are not somewhere exotic in a far-away destination. The destination is right here: where they are. Together as a family, they are having a good time, and enjoying life.

We are all blessed with a family from birth, but we get to choose our friends. Over time, the lines between family and friendships often become blurred as family members become our best friends and friends become our family. Life has meaning when it is shared with others. We are social beings, and it makes us feel good to be surrounded by loving friends and family.

"Come on in," my mother would always say as friends, neighbors, and family members stopped by my parents' house.

"What would you like to eat?" my father would ask as he led the guests to the refrigerator or to the kitchen pantry.

My dad has always loved to stock his kitchen with different kinds of snacks so that whenever friends visited him, he always had something he knew they could enjoy.

Although neither my dad nor my mom ate any of these items, they would always have special chocolate chip cookies for their nephew, or chocolate milk mix for their niece, or peanut butter in the pantry for my children.

My dad's face would light up as he filled the kitchen countertop with snacks on plates for his guests. My mother would brew tea and turn on the stove to make quick home-made "pakoras" (fritters).

It was obvious to me that my parents loved to have guests come to their home, and it was obvious to their guests, too. Whenever guests walked into their home, they felt right at home. As soon as my mom and dad opened the front door, visitors could feel an outpouring of love as my parents hugged them, shook their hands, and scuttled them inside.

I have a long way to go when it comes to entertaining like my parents. I don't know how to whip up home-made snacks like my mother did, and I do not have the luxury of time as they did, but I've learned to find a middle road.

If I am unable to entertain at home, I plan lunches, picnics, concerts, weekend trips, restaurant dinners, and other outings with my friends.

What about you? Why not go call a friend, and make plans for the weekend?

BREATHE

BE STILL

SMILE

Directions for use:

Whenever you feel that stress, anger, or frustration is interfering with your ability to function optimally or whenever you begin to feel disconnected, disjointed, and disorganized, take 60 seconds to create your own little mental oasis, and follow three simple steps:

- **Breathe** – With eyes closed, draw in positive energy, and exhale negative energy. (Slow inhalations and slow exhalations, 20 seconds.)

- **Be still** – Go to the center of your being. (Sitting perfectly still, 20 seconds.)

- **Smile** – Turn all negativity, both internal and external, into positive energy. (Eyes still closed, counting silently to 20 in your mind.)

You can follow these steps as often as once an hour or whenever you feel the need for it. This secret EXECUTIVE YOGI technique can help you maximize your performance and your sense of well-being. Regard this as your own secret SIXTY SECOND mental oasis.

CHAPTER NINE

"The Power Of Two"

CHAPTER NINE

"The Power Of Two"

Northridge, California:

I am sitting in the University library, looking out of the fourth floor window into the calm California night. I am trying to read my macroeconomics textbook, but I cannot concentrate.

I am shocked to realize that I can't read my book because I am thinking about a friend who often studies with me.

"He's just a friend," I tell myself. "Not a boyfriend."

"Then, why am I missing him so much," I ask myself.

"Sure, I admire him, and enjoy his company. He is funny, lively, and full of energy."

"But he's just a friend, right?" I ask myself again."

"Why am I missing him so much?"

I picture his big smile, and his kind dancing eyes.

"Maybe he is more than just a friend," I think.

I am taken by complete surprise.

"When did my feelings change?" I wonder.

I know that he has romantic feelings for me. In fact, he has told me that he is certain that we will marry someday.

"Yeah, sure," I laugh, not taking him seriously.

The first time we met, he had walked into that very library where I am now sitting, and dropped a crimson red rose on my desk. He'd smiled at me with an air of confidence, and then left mysteriously.

This got my attention because the other men I had met at college were often nervous around me.

I didn't even know who he was, and yet, this smiling stranger continued the rose ritual at the library for almost thirty days before he finally asked me out.

We quickly became great friends. We enjoyed talking, walking, and studying together. Sometimes, as we sat talking, we would forget about time and talk for hours.

Now, I am sitting in the library alone and missing him. I realize that I am missing him more than I should be missing him if he were just a friend.

At that moment, someone taps me on the shoulder, bringing me out of my deep thoughts.

It is him. He is standing there, with a wide smile on his face. He has a red rose in one hand and an envelope in the other.

I open the envelope, read the contents, and smile back at him.

At that moment, he and I knew that our friendship had been sealed in love.

THE POWER OF TWO

On the note I read these words:

"Sweet love
Neeti Neeti Dearest
With a heart so earnest
And feelings so finest
Of love let silence be our witness.

Draw near with no fear
To this heart all is clear
To that soul you are too dear
Of love, let silence be our witness.

In friendship no contracts
No succumbing to distracts
No need for alternative tracts
Of love let silence be our witness.

Let this friendship grow
With hearts that glow
And minds that shall flow
Of love let silence be our witness.

Smile my sweet love,
for all the flowers are yours today."

Most of us remember when we fell in love. We felt like we were on the top of the world and nothing could stop us. We had found someone to love and that special someone loved us back.

We were giddy with excitement whenever we had a chance to spend time together, either in person or over the phone. Our faces glowed, and our hearts danced when we saw him or her.

It felt as though all the butterflies in the world had decided to fly around inside our stomachs when our special someone was next to us.

We may have even discovered new talents within ourselves: writing poetry or songs dedicated to the special one.

Unfortunately, we may also remember when we fell out of love.

Okay, not completely out of love. We

still love this person, but we don't feel "in love." Sometimes it may even feel like we are constantly "in fight."

Day-to-day activities like our jobs — which are obviously very important — may get in the way. We do have to make time for work since that is what pays the bills, right?

And, of course, if we are ambitious then we want to do our best work. We want to work on the best projects, which add up to long hours.

When we get home from work, we are often exhausted, and don't make time for our special someone. If we do make time, we may be short tempered, impatient, and argumentative. There are probably also times when irritability leads to arguments. Afterwards we may not even remember what the argument was about.

A happy personal relationship at home and excellence in our career are not mutually exclusive. They can go hand in hand. All it takes is the right mindset.

At work, we have a plan for each day. We have a timeline for each project. We probably also have a deadline to complete projects.

The same should apply to our personal relationships.

If things could be better in our relationships, we might want to ask ourselves what we can do to make our special person feel "special!"

I like to make a project list, and give myself a deadline for each week.

These projects do not have to be grandiose or expensive.

When I focus on this one simple question — "What can I do to show my affection?" — I come up with many different ways to make my "love" feel special. And, surprisingly, these actions don't take much time.

Little doses of loving action on a regular basis reach deep into the heart and leave a mark forever.

His eyes are shining, and his face is expanding into a smile he can't hold back. He gazes expectantly at me.

"When do I get to redeem my gift certificate, love?" my husband keeps asking me.

He is like a small child who can't wait to open a Christmas gift. I have given him a hand-made gift certificate for Father's Day.

It reads:

> "Thanks for being a loving and caring dad to our two beautiful children. You are a great role model for them. To honor your contributions as the father to our family, I present you this gift certificate today. You may redeem it for a massage by your wife. When: Anytime this week."

All it takes is a little planning to infuse our "so very busy" lives with care, love, and joy.

My husband and I have a morning ritual.

If I have to wake up at 4 am, I set the alarm for 3:50 am instead.

When the alarm goes off, I crawl out of bed, and reset the alarm for 4 am. I then get right back into bed.

Those next ten minutes are the most important part of our lives because they set the tone for the rest of the day. The ten minutes are part of what we call "hug time."

Each morning, when the "Hug Alarm" goes off, we turn over and hug each other. Even if we had a little argument the night before and don't feel like hugging, we simply do.

It is funny what happens to our feelings when we start hugging. Any anger or frustration simply evaporates away. The love that we have for each other washes over every cell of the body. Now, when the true "wake up alarm" goes off, we literally spring out of bed ready to enjoy the day.

We all face the challenge of time. We put in a full day at work, and by the time we come home, there's little time left in the day. Dinner, dishes, children, putting clothes away, planning the next day, watching a little television, or reading a book, and the only thing we want to do is put our heads on our pillows and fall asleep.

Is that any way to end the day? No, especially if we have our special person there with us. We should TALK to each other, and share the happenings of the day. It will make us feel closer.

This is the person who is our best friend, the person with whom we can't wait to share everything that is on our mind. There are times when we put our head on this person's shoulder for strength when life hasn't treated us well.

We should think of marriage as a perpetual date — a good date that never comes to an end. When you were dating your spouse, or if you are not married and are still dating, I am sure you take the time to plan the date. You think about where you will go, what you will do, what you will wear, and even what you might say.

The same goes for marriage. Take the time to dress up and look nice, feel good, and be sweet. This is the most important person in your world.

We always try to give our best at work whether we are in a bad mood or under the weather. We are able to override these challenges at work and do what is required of us. We should do the same when it comes to our spouse or loved one.

When we are invited to someone's house, we take the time to look presentable. We should do the same when it comes to our spouse. Make it a ritual to wear something "appealing." We all have different tastes. It really doesn't matter what we wear, as long as it is something we are comfortable in and our spouse finds it attractive.

There are times when we come home and we are so tired that even the thought of talking seems tiresome. However, have you noticed that when we toss aside the idea of how tired we are and focus on having a heart-warming evening with each other, we tend to forget about the rest of the day?

We feel energized, loving, and content. We should make it a habit to show each other our love. What a wonderful way this is to end an evening and start the next day.

My husband walked in the door after work one day. I heard him say, "Honey, can you please make me a cup of chai?"

He looked completely worn out from his long day at work, and I wanted him to feel better.

I reached out to give him a hug, but a little voice inside my mind jumped in:

"I've just come home from a long day at work myself, and I, too, am tired. He should make his own tea."

And, I'm sorry to say, that is exactly what I said to my husband.

I felt a little ashamed as I heard him making his own tea.

Later, as I reflected back on my reaction to my husband's modest request, I realized how silly and self-centered I had been. All he had asked for was a cup of tea. It would have taken me less than two minutes to make it.

Instead of pointing out that we both work, and that he was capable of making his own tea, I realized that, YES, he knows how to make tea. He makes tea for himself all the time.

It wasn't really that he didn't have the knowledge or the energy to make the tea: when he asked me to make him a cup of tea, he was asking for me to show him my love for him. Pure and simple. And, I had squandered an opportunity to make the most important person in my life feel loved when he came home.

I felt even worse the more I thought about it. When I've had a bad day and need "tender loving care," my husband goes out of his way to make me feel like a queen.

Since the "chai incident," I've learned to ignore the "selfish voice" in my head and take action from my heart.

Most days, I leave for work before my husband does. He always walks me to my car. He carries my briefcase, and places it in the back seat. He then opens the car for me.

I can certainly open my own car door and carry my own briefcase, but that extra attention from my husband in the morning goes a long way. It shows me that he loves and values me.

This action takes him no longer than two minutes, but it leaves a "stamp of love" in my heart. Let me tell you, this is a really big and deep stamp.

We should always make sure to stamp our love on our loved ones everyday. To do that, we must find out what they would like us to do for them.

How we speak to our loved ones is also important. Addressing our loved ones in a loving manner reinforces how we feel about them.

I have noticed that anytime my husband calls me on the phone, he usually starts his sentence with "Hi Love," or "Hey Beautiful." When our loved ones start a conversation in this manner, it is hard to fight them even when we may be tempted to.

It is also important for us to remember special days — especially anniversaries and birthdays. We shouldn't let these special occasions go by without celebrating even if we must work late that day.

We can buy a special card, or handwrite a love note. We can bring home a favorite dessert, a gift, or even do something as simple as light candles on the dinner table. For special occasions, we should make every effort to get home so we can enjoy a nice dinner with our loved ones. Come on, we are talking about five or six days out of the whole year. We should always make it a habit to be home on time for dinner as often as possible.

If we want our loved ones to make us feel special, we should make it easy for them by telling them what we like or dislike. I learned this one year on my birthday, when my darling husband brought home chocolate pudding instead of a cake for my birthday. I do not like chocolate pudding on any day of the week, but certainly not for a special event like my birthday.

After the "chocolate pudding incident," as I think of it, I gave my husband a list of what I like and enjoy. He knows that if he runs out of ideas, he can refer to my list and easily please me with gifts of vanilla or pistachio ice-cream, flowers, books, music, pens, crystal jewelry, or tickets to a concert.

Even if we are not very imaginative, and we can't afford to be extravagant, we can still step out of our normal routine once in a while. We can do something larger than life that our loved ones will remember.

"These are gorgeous!" I squealed as the florist delivered two dozen red roses to my office. I could feel tears starting to well up in my eyes as I tried to contain my excitement. I pulled the card off the bouquet, knowing before I read it that the roses were from my husband.

On the card were written these words:

> "For my WIFE, because you are my LIFE."

He knew I'd been working on a very tough project that would be going on all week, and that I'd been feeling a little down.

How could I feel down when surrounded by two dozen red roses? He knew exactly what to do to make me feel wonderful.

I can still picture those roses, and recall their sweet fragrance. That day is anchored in my head and heart.

On occasions when I become irritated with my husband, I make it a point to remember that day and let it take over my heart. Loving feelings quickly replace the temporary annoyance.

We should all create "love-anchors" in our lives. In even the most loving relationships, every single day is not going to be perfect. We need "love anchors" to hold us in place when the tide is high and threatens to sweep our love away.

Instead of having lunch with a co-worker or eating at our desk, we can make a lunch date with our loved ones, or meet them for a happy hour. Most importantly, we should thank them for joining us for lunch, just like we would thank anyone else. It is funny how we tend to take for granted the ones we care about the most.

The simplest way to show our loved ones that we care is through a touch, hug, or kiss each time we say goodnight or good-bye. It is just another way to connect. If we do it often enough, it becomes a habit. Another anchor.

Whenever my husband travels out of town, the one thing I miss most about him is our morning good-bye kiss when he walks me to the car. It is the little habits and rituals we create in our day-to-day life that keeps us powerfully connected to our loved ones, especially when they are away.

We should be open. We should share moments with each other — tough moments and happy moments. We should not wait until we get a big promotion or a big raise to spend more time together, or do something special.

We can pull out the treasures of photos, cards, and poetry from the early days of our relationship. My husband and I used to write poetry to each other, and one night I was reading some of it aloud to him, just for fun.

"If you read anymore, I am going to die laughing," he gasped.

Laughter and sweet memories of the past are both powerful love anchors.

We should take the time and care to infuse our relationship with affection, compassion, and respect. It isn't enough to say the words "I love you."

We also need to make the spoken words real by acting in loving ways.

We all have different ways of showing our love. My grandparents never showed any affection toward each other in public. I never saw them hold hands or even give each other a little hug. Yet, their love for each other was undeniably there through their sixty-five years of marriage. I could see in the ways they looked at each other, and in the shared hopes, dreams, and aspirations they had for their children and grandchildren.

Kaiser Hospital, Woodland Hills, California:

The family is gathered in the hospital room where my grandfather is hooked to monitors and wires. My mind wanders to the times when he used to take me to puppet shows when I was little. Today, he looks more like one of those puppets, performing the dance of life and death with the doctors and nurses, than my strong grandpa.

Now, lying in the hospital bed he looks like a punctured tire that is deflating slowly. It is hard to believe that this frail man is the same man who has always been my hero.

The room feels of imminent death. I can hear my own heartbeat.

I can almost hear and feel his heartbeat…or so I hope. The doctor comes in and tells us there is little time left and that we should prepare to say our good-byes to him.

I look at my grandmother, who is about to lose her husband, her companion, and her soul mate. My eyes fill with tears.

I see my grandmother move away from my grandfather to the very corner of the room. I ask her to move closer as I make room for her next to his bedside.

She shakes her head and simply says, "No, no, 'Beta' (daughter), I am fine here. It is better this way for me and for him. Your grandfather is in a lot of physical pain, and I do not want to prolong this pain for him. If I move away, he cannot see my emotional pain and my fear of losing him. It will be easier for him to 'let go' and move on."

Such was my grandparents' love for each other. Unspoken, yet put into practice till the day they parted.

When King Shah Jahan's wife, Mumtaz, passed away in India, he built the magnificent Taj Mahal in her memory.

We don't need to build anything of such a monumental nature, but what is important is that we build memories and special moments with each other while we are together.

We should remember to:

- Cherish each other.

- Create feelings of mutual respect and love.

- Be best friends to each other.

BREATHE

BE STILL

SMILE

Directions for use:

Whenever you feel that stress, anger, or frustration is interfering with your ability to function optimally or whenever you begin to feel disconnected, disjointed, and disorganized, take 60 seconds to create your own little mental oasis, and follow three simple steps:

- **Breathe** – With eyes closed, draw in positive energy, and exhale negative energy. (Slow inhalations and slow exhalations, 20 seconds.)

- **Be still** – Go to the center of your being. (Sitting perfectly still, 20 seconds.)

- **Smile** – Turn all negativity, both internal and external, into positive energy. (Eyes still closed, counting silently to 20 in your mind.)

You can follow these steps as often as once an hour or whenever you feel the need for it. This secret EXECUTIVE YOGI technique can help you maximize your performance and your sense of well-being. Regard this as your own secret SIXTY SECOND mental oasis.

CHAPTER TEN

"The Power Of Family"

CHAPTER TEN

"The Power Of Family"

We all think our children are beautiful, and they are. There's something about their innocence that touches our hearts. Is it the way they look at us through adorable eyes with undying admiration, as if we are the center of their world?

We are their first care-takers who provide for most of their physical and emotional needs. As they grow older, they may not need us to take of them physically, but they still look to us for guidance.

Kaiser Hospital Emergency Ward, Woodland Hills, California:

My little one-year-old darling daughter is
suffering from an allergic reaction to peni-
cillin. Her breathing is compromised. The
doctors are treating her, but so far, her lungs
are not responding.

I am sitting in the hospital, holding her
close to my heart. It feels like a team of
drummers are beating on a thousand drums
inside the room.

My head is pounding and my heart is
beating so hard it feels like it might bounce
right out of my chest. Every cell in my
body aches. The back of my neck is knotted
and tight.

I look down at my precious baby. Her
little face is so pale that it blends in with the
cream hospital bed sheets she is lying on.
Her normally bright and playful eyes are

fading away just like a flashlight which starts blinking on and off right before its batteries finally give up.

"We have done everything we can do," the doctor says. "Hopefully this medication will work and her lungs will respond. Now, we can only wait, and hope."

"What is he saying?" I think. "I can't lose my precious little baby."

Memories flash through my mind:

- The pure love that swept over me — so powerful that it almost caught me by surprise — when the nurse handed her to me the day she was born.

- The beautiful smiles she gives me when I come home from work.

- The feeling of her little heart beating against mine when I hold her.

- The way she snuggles in between my husband and me when we are sitting on the couch together.

- The sound of her first uninhibited

and boisterous laughter when her
cousin sang a silly song for her.

I can no longer hold back my tears. I begin to sob uncontrollably. My husband takes
me in his arms and holds me tight.

"Honey, you have to be strong," he says.
"If you break down now, you are not going to help our baby. We don't know if the
medication will work, but we have to hope
for the best. Our baby is still here with us,
so let us spend this precious time with her."

Through my tears, I look over at our
daughter, and she gives me a weak smile, as
if saying, "Mommy, don't cry."

My precious baby is fighting for each
breath, and yet, she still finds the energy to
smile at me. "I must pull myself together,"
I tell myself. I dry my tears and hold my
daughter close. She wraps her little fingers
tightly around me.

My husband in turn holds me tight, and
our three year old son is clinging to my husband, not fully understanding what is going
on. Our little "Kitty," as we call our daughter,

is fighting back with all her one-year-old might and strength.

We sit like this — all four of us — through the long terrible night. The darkness of the sky seems to fill our hearts, but when the sun comes up, the crisis has passed. Our little "Kitty" is breathing normally.

This experience changed me. It wasn't that I hadn't known before how much I loved my daughter and son, but that night taught me the importance of valuing each moment of each day. I pledged to myself that I would cherish each day with my children.

As parents, grand parents, uncles, aunts, teachers, and mentors, it is our responsibility to provide the mental nourishment to children. Children need it just like they need nutritional meals and vitamins to grow into healthy adults. The emotional loving and guiding is even more important than the physical care-taking.

We are entrusted with the responsibility of shaping another human being's life. That is not something we should take lightly. What we do today for our children, with our children, and in the presence of our children will leave an imprint on them forever.

Let's be sure to make it a positive imprint, which in turn will lead them to be caring, loving, and happy adults.

Many of us work outside the home, and it can be difficult to spend quality time with our children when we come home, tired from a long day at work. Some of us work inside the home, which can be just as challenging. We must realize that it is sometimes the little things we can do that will make all the difference in a child's life.

We plan out our days at work. We make lists of chores to run for the house. We should also plan activities with our children, and when we are with them, we should envelope them in our love and caring.

Reading and storytelling is a great way to connect with children. I have never met a child who did not like listening to a good story.

Town of Ranchi, India:

It is five-thirty in the evening. People in my town are already on their way home from work. I am standing on the balcony, peering down the bend in the street. I am stretching my neck like a little giraffe, trying to catch sight of my dad.

Today is a special day because it is the last day of the month, the day when my dad receives his paycheck. I know that he will be bringing home new books for my brother and me.

I see my dad drive up to the gate of the house, and I race down the stairs to see him, bounding three steps at a time. He hands me the precious package and I scan the title: "*Little Women.*"

I thank him and rush up to my room because I cannot wait to start reading.

I already have quite a collection of books proudly displayed in my bedroom. Without ever forcing my brother and me to read, this wonderful man has given us a love of books and reading.

I read a few chapters, and then it is dinner time. I'm excited, but my excitement has nothing to do with food. My excitement is related to the "dinner ritual" that accompanies the food.

Yes, my mother will serve delicious "gobi-aaloo" (cauliflower with potatoes) or other fresh vegetables, steaming "moong daal" (lentils), and freshly made "rotis" (Indian flat bread) with a touch of "ghee" (homemade pure butter). But best of all, with the food, will come stories about my mother's day.

She has a round smiling face. Her hair is parted in the middle, pulled back in a loose ponytail and she wears a "bindi" (red dot) on her wide forehead that matches the color of her bright sari.

She serves the food and then her animated voice begins to tell us about the neighbor who has just returned from an exotic vacation, the guests that "Mrs. A" had from abroad, or a story she has read in a magazine that day.

My little brother and I listen — wide eyed — to her stories, because to us they are no less than adventures of a superhero. We both adore her.

Although she is talking directly to my dad, she always ends each story with a lesson to be learned — a lesson that is aimed at my brother and me.

Through my mother's daily story-telling, my brother and I learn many of the life lessons that every child needs. The stories stick in our brains because she does not lecture us, but creatively teaches us about life, love, morals, and ethics through her stories.

We listen, and we learn.

Once my mother's stories are done, my father takes over with his story-telling. Sometimes my father tells us stories written by authors, and other times, he makes them up as he goes along.

When my brother and I complain about the veggies we must eat, my dad's story stops. He tells us that the story will only begin again if we do not complain about our food.

Tonight my dad is telling my favorite story of all, a story that was written by a children's author. It is called "The Monkey and the Hat Vendor." In the story, the hat vendor sits under a tree to rest. When he wakes up, he sees that the monkeys who live in the tree have stolen all his hats.

He begs, pleads, and even throws stones at the monkeys, but they do not want to relinquish the hats. At last, the vendor decides to use his brain. Knowing that monkeys love to copy others, the vendor takes his own hat off his head, and throws it on the ground. Lo and behold, the next thing he knows, all the monkeys take their hats off and throw them down on the ground. He gathers up the hats and goes on his way.

My dad follows this story with one he makes up. It is about an evil witch, who lives among humans. The only way you can tell her apart from other people is by looking at her feet, which are on backwards!

Now, I tell my children these same stories. I also teach them to love reading books. Their bookshelves are filled with books: The Hardy Boys Series (which used to be one of my favorite book series as a child), short story collections, the classics, books about dinosaurs and volcanoes, and books about how things work.

My mother-in-law also tells my children stories about her days spent in a small town called Bukumbi, which is located in Tanzania, East Africa. She describes her encounters with a wild deer, who once charged at her as she held onto her terrified son (my husband). She also has stories about the wild brightly-colored parrots that flew by their house, or the slithering and deadly mamba snake that almost bit my husband in the Serengeti. The children love these stories, and beg her to recount them again and again.

My husband has a whole series of stories about the five horses, which live on a farm. These stories evolve, with the horses taking on new adventures to fit the life lessons we want the children to learn.

The lessons we all weave into our stories include these:

- Respecting parents.

- Honoring grandparents and other elders.

- Being kind and loving to siblings.

- Eating healthy.

- Striving to do our best in everything.

- Doing the right thing even when we don't feel like it.

- Following a routine.

- Having a discipline in life.

- Reading.

- Remembering to say "Thank you" and "Please."

- Having fun in life.

- Not just loving, but showing love through words and actions.

- Apologizing when we make a mistake.

It is also important to me that my two children grow up to be close to each other and foster a deep loving relationship. When I see them being nice to each other, I constantly tell them: "Both of you will be inseparable when you grow up, and your families in turn will be very close to each other."

My children do sometimes fight with each other because they are very different individuals, but what I notice most is that they indeed are very close.

In our family, we celebrate "Rakhi." This is an Indian tradition in which a brother and a sister reaffirm their love and caring for each other once a year.

The sister ties a thread or "rakhi" on her brother's wrist to signify the "bond of love" which will now hold them together for ever. The brother in turn gives her a gift (yes, women all over the world love to get gifts) and vows to take care of her, protect her, and love her until his last breath on earth.

Despite that pledge and their affection for each other, my children sometimes argue, and my son is sometimes embarrassed by his little sister.

I remember one day when my daughter was twirling in her sleeveless pink dress with bright yellow flowers on the front. She wanted to show off the new dress she had received as a gift from my son.

She stopped and enveloped "Bhai" (Big Brother) in a loving hug while he made a face at her, saying, "Yuck…get away."

Even though my son sometimes fights with his sister, he will not allow anyone else to do anything that will upset her. He watches over her with utmost love and caring like a protective hawk with a chick.

Let me tell you another story. My daughter and son used to travel to school on the same bus. A bully on the bus had been mean to my daughter by constantly teasing her.

One day, the bully shouted at her in a very loud and harsh voice that made her cry. My son, two years younger than the bully, stood up and had the courage to tell the boy not to mess with his sister.

My daughter came running home after the bus dropped her off at the house. Instead of being upset and recalling how mean that boy had been to her, her focus was on a heartwarming story she shared with me.

"Mommy," she said. "Brother told the mean boy to back off, and then he hugged me until I stopped crying. Mom, don't say anything to him because he'll be embarrassed."

I watched my son as he climbed off the bus and sauntered to our front door, nonchalant, as if nothing had happened. I was so proud of him. The big brother had indeed learned the real meaning behind the tradition of "Rakhi" and was looking out for his sister. She in turn had gained a new-found respect and adoration for him.

Children are full of energy and as parents, it is our duty to harness that energy and channel it into positive activities. What has worked well for our family is to schedule different fun activities for each day of the week.

As a family, we sit down and make a list, which may include: Walking, dancing, reading, storytelling, watching a movie, watching TV, going to the park, reading poetry, making up stories or poetry, painting, drawing, playing video games or making a snack together.

When we choose an activity like reading for the evening, we finish our dinner and then we retire to the family room. Each of us has a book in hand, ready to be swept deep into the stories we are reading. We play some music in the background.

Depending upon the mood of the family, as we read, we listen to old disco songs, Indian bhangra (music with drums), Latin, classical, or a variety of music from different countries. The children not only enjoy reading but are simultaneously exposed to music from various cultural backgrounds. My husband and I get to enjoy a quiet and relaxing evening with the children.

"I can't believe they are actually enjoying reading," I often whisper to my husband as I glance toward my children engrossed in their books.

Of course, there are evenings when we simply want to focus on ourselves, our activities, and our interests. As our children get a little older, we can involve them in our activities. For the most part, children don't care what they do with us, as long as they get to do it with us.

My husband spends a lot of time on his computer following the movements of the stock market and researching the real estate market. He has designated our son as his "Real Estate Intern" and our daughter as his "Stock Market Intern." They are thrilled with their titles.

When my husband prepares to study the real estate market, he has my son sit next to him and explains to him what he is researching and why. When he works on our stock portfolio, he in turn explains to our daughter how the market works and what drives the stock price of public companies.

She has learned to use his stock charting software and helps drive the analysis, whereas our son provides his valued opinion on different properties or timeshares. I call this a true "win-win" situation.

My husband spends time doing what he enjoys. The children get to spend valuable one-on-one time with their father, while at the same time learning important financial skills for the future and contributing their opinion as valued members of the family.

Besides practical life skills, it is also important that children learn personal responsibility. In order to encourage responsible behavior, we helped the children create a daily and weekly responsibility list which is taped to the refrigerator.

Items on this list include completing homework without being told, getting school bags and lunch bags ready for next day, cleaning their rooms before going to bed, brushing teeth at night, saying their prayers, and giving a nightly hug to their parents: us!

Each child has a space next to these items to place a check mark if that goal is accomplished. They earn a point for each activity completed without supervision. It is quite a sight to see them rushing to the refrigerator to check off their activities. It has created a healthy competition between the two children.

The children also helped craft a mission statement for the family. In this statement, we affirm our love and caring for each other while helping each other grow to our fullest potential. This statement describes the family members and their hobbies, interests, and dreams. What we have noticed is that the statement has continued to change and evolve as each family member has — in turn — changed over time.

When my son was two years old, he loved to sing songs with his toy guitar hanging from his neck. He learned classic songs from his grandmother and would entertain us for hours.

Now, his interests have turned to video games, creating websites, drawing cartoon characters, making and telling jokes (yes, he is very funny), and editing and publishing a weekly magazine he created for his class. He wants to design gaming software and produce movies when he grows up.

My daughter enjoys dancing, singing, reading, and watching Discovery Channel shows about animals. She wants to be a veterinarian or a doctor when she grows up. Regardless of our children's interests (often very different from our own), we love to encourage them.

Children will be children and will not fit into our perfect and ideal vision at all times. On those not-so-perfect occasions, it is important that we remind the children (and ourselves also) of the times when the children have behaved well and that that is the behavior that is expected from them.

As they grow up, it will be up to them to decide how they will live their lives. Hopefully what they learned from us will stick with them and they will make the right decisions as they go through life. We must always try to do the best we can as parents and grand parents to instill the right qualities, morals, and values in our children and grand-children.

A beautiful resort in Palm Springs, California:

My husband and I are enjoying a cup of steaming hot, but stale "bitter-lobby-coffee" as we stretch out on the well-worn, but comfortable love seat. The children are playing video games in the resort game room.

I am wondering if my husband and I are doing "okay" as parents compared to how our own parents had raised us.

I hear a woman's voice calling our name. Her booming voice reverberates against the lobby walls and echoes back.

A petite, well-dressed, and serious-looking woman is striding toward us.

"Are you the parents of those children?" she asks.

"Now what?" I think.

My husband and I look at each other and then nod, and say, "Yes."

"I just had to stop and share this with you," she says. "Your children are exceptionally well-behaved. I work at the front desk and your two children came by earlier today to check out videos. They stood in line quietly, and when it was their turn, they politely asked for the movie list and said thank you when I gave them their movies. Such nice children!"

The next night, we are eating a nice sea-food dinner in a restaurant.

Our waitress says, "You have such good children. I couldn't help noticing how nicely they have been sitting and eating with you, talking to you, and enjoying their meal."

With a sweet smile on her face, she says she is pleased to serve them because they treat her politely and with respect.

I can barely look at her. I have to turn my face away because my eyes are starting to drip-drip-drip tears. I let my husband respond to the waitress while I pretend to have something in my eyes while I wipe my "proud-mommy-tears" away.

The biggest gift we can give to our children as parents is to be happy individuals. If we are happy, our children have a better chance of being happy. We can show our love for them by keeping a happy and smiling persona.

"Mommy," my son often says to me. "I am so happy when you are happy."

He loves it when I watch a television show with him, and we laugh heartily together. I notice that he concentrates more on me laughing my head off than watching the show.

He also enjoys hearing stories about himself, like this one:

He was a very fussy baby, and it used to take a long time to feed him even two ounces of milk at a time. One day, I was going to be late from work due to a dinner meeting. In preparation for the evening away from home, I had left a bottle of breast milk in a container in the refrigerator.

Before leaving the house that morning, I gave specific instructions to my husband about our son's feeding times for the evening.

When I arrived home late in the night, my husband told me that our son did not give him any problems in drinking his milk bottle, and that he had, in fact, consumed six ounces of milk in one sitting. With a playful smirk on his face, my husband said that he was obviously better at feeding our son than I was.

Imagine my surprise when I opened the refrigerator and noticed that more than half the breast milk was still in its container. I asked my husband to show me what he had fed our son.

He pointed to evaporated canned milk. My jaw dropped! No wonder the baby had gulped it down. It was sweet and yummy, unlike the bland breast milk he was used to drinking.

The story gets even better. My husband normally uses the canned milk as creamer in his tea. Now, it was time for his jaw to drop when he realized that he had had two cups of delicious English tea that evening with breast-milk in them. My son and I still tease him about his "special tea" as we collapse in fits of laughter.

All of us as parents want the best for our children. We enjoy spending time with them, but we also need our own time to recharge. When I come home from work, I greet the children with a tight hug. But after that, they know that they must adhere to the "ten-minute rule." For ten minutes, mommy needs to be left alone while she sips from a cup of tea.

That window of personal time helps me to distance my thoughts from work and transition into the "mommy and wife role." I flip through the news, or thumb through the latest issues of Vogue, Harvard Business Review, or Architectural Digest. I am then ready to take on the evening.

After the ten-minute time frame, the children come rushing to share stories about their day, or pull me into their rooms to show me a website they may have created, or a new "tight" song they may have downloaded to their i-pods. (It took me a while to understand that "tight" means "cool" in their school slang.)

Each of us is different. Each family has different dynamics and interests. Figure out what works for you and your children. Just as a yogi sets aside time for introspection, set aside time to think through what you and your children enjoy doing together.

What values do we want to foster in them? How would we like to see them five years from today? Ten years from today? As adults? As parents to their own children, our future grandchildren? What we do in this moment will shape their lives today and their children's lives tomorrow.

We should jot down the things we enjoy together and do more of it. We should smile more often, and gather our children into our arms for no reason.

BREATHE

BE STILL

SMILE

Directions for use:

Whenever you feel that stress, anger, or frustration is interfering with your ability to function optimally or whenever you begin to feel disconnected, disjointed, and disorganized, take 60 seconds to create your own little mental oasis, and follow three simple steps:

- **Breathe** – With eyes closed, draw in positive energy, and exhale negative energy. (Slow inhalations and slow exhalations, 20 seconds.)

- **Be still** – Go to the center of your being. (Sitting perfectly still, 20 seconds.)

- **Smile** – Turn all negativity, both internal and external, into positive energy. (Eyes still closed, counting silently to 20 in your mind.)

You can follow these steps as often as once an hour or whenever you feel the need for it. This secret EXECUTIVE YOGI technique can help you maximize your performance and your sense of well-being. Regard this as your own secret SIXTY SECOND mental oasis.

CHAPTER ELEVEN

"The Power Of Giving"

CHAPTER ELEVEN

"The Power Of Giving"

At the home of "Bowji" (Grandpa) and
"Biji" (Grandma) in Agra, India:

My family has recently moved from the
town of Ranchi to the city of Agra to live
with my grandparents.

The temple and church bells are calling everyone to action. Everyone is up and
about in the Dewan Household. The adults
are getting ready to go to work and the children are packing their school bags, ready to
dash to the bus stop for the start of another
school day. It is a typical hectic morning.

I see Grandma is in the kitchen. She
is directing the cooking of a feast for over
two hundred people. One servant is chop-
ping the vegetables while another is grating
ginger, garlic, and turmeric (the three basic
ingredients in any Indian curry).

Grandma is boiling "basmati" rice for both the rice pilaf and the "rice kheer" (rice pudding). My mother is kneading the dough from which she will help make "rotis" (fresh flat bread).

This special meal for two hundred people is not for a private party of friends and family. It is for a "langar" (also referred to as "The Open Lunch Kitchen") at the local temple we often attend. Today Grandma and Grandpa are the sponsors of the lunch.

It is a long-standing Indian tradition to provide free food to anyone who comes to the temple at lunch time, regardless of their religion, race, or social status. All the temple-goers will sit together and enjoy the food that has been provided by the sponsoring family of the day.

I stop and ask my mom if I can miss school today. I want to be involved in this exciting venture and help my grandmother and mother. Upon hearing my request, they look at each other and laugh.

My mother says, "Neeti, we know you just want to get your hands dirty in the wheat flour and make a mess." They deny my request and tell me to get going or I'll be late for school.

I rush out with my school bag slung across my shoulder, and sprint to meet the "tanga" (horse-carriage) that will take me to school. The "tanga man" (horse-carriage driver) helps me onto the seat.

He makes a "click-click" sound with his mouth, which signals the horse to start galloping. We make our way to school, surrounded by other "tangas," bicycles, cars, scooters, mopeds, and even cows.

On the way to school, my horse-carriage passes the temple. I notice the temple-goers. Some are rich and others are poor. The rich are dressed in designer outfits while the poor are in hand-me-down tattered clothes. Some are stepping out of their chauffer-driven cars while others walk barefoot from their neighboring dirt huts.

I know that when my grandmother and mother come to the temple to serve the food they are preparing, it won't matter who the temple-goers are or where they come from.

Some of the temple-goers are used to dining in the finest restaurants and private clubs. They will view the "langar" as an additional snack in their well-fed day.

Others will come to the temple and enjoy the hearty "langar" as their only full meal of the day.

Today at this special lunch, I know that they will ALL (rich and poor) eat the same food, seated together as part of one community.

Many of us in the United States have never had to go hungry for a day, let alone an hour! Most of us have been blessed to have a shelter over our heads and food on the table, even in dire times when we may have been temporarily unemployed or when we had an unexpected sickness in the family.

There are times when I wonder if what I have is enough, and I recall the grateful faces of some of the poor temple-goers. For them, "langar" time in the temple was the only time in a whole day when they were able to enjoy a full meal.

But there is also a cautionary tale here for us. We should not take our jobs or our income for granted. As we generate income, we should make a point of not just earning wealth, but also preserving and growing it for the future.

A good rule of thumb is to put away a minimum of ten percent of our gross earnings, and then watch our nest egg grow. Compound interest is a very impressive savings tool. Before we know it, our ten percent begins to multiply and grow significantly.

All of us have different tolerance for risk. We need to sit down with a financial advisor, family members, and a good accountant and decide what works for us.

We can invest our savings across the board: in stocks, bonds, mutual funds, or real estate. It is important that we save for the future and have a portfolio of investments.

Just like yogis spend time on self assessment, we can also put aside time to assess how our portfolio is performing. We should periodically review it and determine if we need to make any changes. It is also beneficial to involve the family in these decisions so that each family member is aware of the family's finances.

While accumulating and preserving wealth is important, it is also important that we spend wealth judiciously and enjoy it. What is the point of wealth if we don't use it?

We should set aside some of our wealth every month for fun. We can schedule a beautiful family vacation, throw a party for friends or family, enjoy a good massage, purchase a dress, or a set of weights.

It is also important that we use our wealth to help others. We should all make it a point to pledge money, time, and talent to charity.

Burbank, California:

I am rushing across the parking lot of the Walgreen's drugstore. I am in a rush to develop the pictures from our family's latest vacation in Cabo San Lucas, Mexico.

I think I hear a voice calling to me, but I'm not sure. I turn my head to look around, and notice a hand with knotted knuckles waving frantically from the rolled-down window of a nearby car.

"Here, young lady, here!" I hear an old woman shout.

I stride toward the red Cadillac that is parked in the handicapped zone.

"I've been calling out for the last half hour, hoping that someone would come to help me get out of the car. I am so glad you are here," she mutters in relief.

She tells me that she suffers from multiple sclerosis and needs a hand getting out of her car. Once she is out of the car, she can pull her walker from the back seat, and make her way to the drugstore. I help her get out of her car and walk with her to the drug store.

"Sweetheart," she says to me, once we are inside the Walgreens. "God bless you for stopping to help me. I used to be young and vibrant like you, and now look at me! Enjoy your life while you have your health and youth. By the way, thanks again, sweetie!"

I didn't do anything more than spend an extra minute or two with this woman, and offer her my hand. I realized that she had helped me more than I had helped her because she had left me with a very powerful message.

The message is a very simple one, and one that we should think about every day: We should not take good health for granted. We should make sure to experience life fully.

Living life fully is all wealth is for. Money in itself has no meaning. It is only a tool to be used to help ourselves, our families, and the wider community.

BREATHE

BE STILL

SMILE

Directions for use:

Whenever you feel that stress, anger, or frustration is interfering with your ability to function optimally or whenever you begin to feel disconnected, disjointed, and disorganized, take 60 seconds to create your own little mental oasis, and follow three simple steps:

- **Breathe** – With eyes closed, draw in positive energy, and exhale negative energy. (Slow inhalations and slow exhalations, 20 seconds.)

- **Be still** – Go to the center of your being. (Sitting perfectly still, 20 seconds.)

- **Smile** – Turn all negativity, both internal and external, into positive energy. (Eyes still closed, counting silently to 20 in your mind.)

You can follow these steps as often as once an hour or whenever you feel the need for it. This secret EXECUTIVE YOGI technique can help you maximize your performance and your sense of well-being. Regard this as your own secret SIXTY SECOND mental oasis.

CHAPTER TWELVE

"The Power Of Goodness"

CHAPTER TWELVE

"The Power Of Goodness"

Life is a precious gift bestowed upon
us. We must learn to make the most of it
for ourselves and for others. We are here to
learn, grow, evolve, and to better ourselves
and this world.

To do this, we must take responsibility
for our lives and take it upon ourselves to be
leaders so that we can leave behind a legacy
of love, laughter, and joy as well as a legacy
of personal and public improvement.

Even though a faraway star may be de-
stroyed, its brilliant light continues to travel
toward earth. Our eyes cannot tell the difference between the light that shines in the
sky from a star that is still present today or
from one that burned itself out eons ago.
That is a fascinating fact. Such is also true
of our individual legacies.

What will our legacies be?

Each of us is endowed with special gifts and talents. Each of us matters. What we do today and create in our lives will continue to influence and touch the lives of people even when we are no longer present. Our children, friends, co-workers, and family are affected by our temperament, actions, and thoughts. Let these all be positive influences.

Just like the brilliance of faraway stars, positive influences stay with us forever. I remember such a positive influence in my own life. Her name was Mrs. Kamal Thakur, my sixth grade teacher.

Growing up in India, I attended Sacred Heart School, a Roman Catholic school for girls. At the beginning of 6th Grade, I was elected class captain. As captain of my class, it was my job to help maintain discipline and lead the class in inter-class competitions.

One day, my class was getting somewhat wild. A few classmates had opened the wide wall-to-wall windows and were peering out into the basketball court. While we waited for our next teacher to arrive, we were required to stand quietly at our desks.

When the teachers entered the classroom, we would grab our skirts on the ends and bow down with a greeting: "Good Morning" (or "Good Afternoon") Mrs. Thakur." This day was not one of those quiet days.

In order to bring control back in the classroom, I came down hard on the rowdy students. The room was finally quiet. Discipline was restored. But, my classmates, who were also my friends, were upset with me. They complained that I was turning my back on them and I was no longer a part of their team. Finally, I broke down and ran out of the classroom to Mrs. Thakur's school office and cried.

"I don't want to be the leader anymore," I sobbed. "It's too tough. I just want to be part of my group."

She looked at me and said, "Neeti, leaders have to be tough sometimes. You have to stand up for what is right, even if that is not the popular opinion. Now, go back in there and face your classmates. Do your job of being a good leader. I don't want to hear abut you wanting to quit. Not today. Not ever!"

Later that year, our class was named the "Best Behaved Class of the Year." I was happy. All my classmates were happy. Our teacher was proud of us. I never forgot Mrs. Thakur's words. Her wisdom will always stay with me. As I go through life and run into difficult situations, I recall her words about what a leader stands for.

We must realize that no matter what our role, we are all leaders to those around us. Whether we are leading in a positive or negative direction is up to us. We can choose to stand up for what is right in life. We can focus on what we can do to create positive influences, especially on those who are close to us.

I always set aside SIXTY SECONDS in the early morning, and again before I go to sleep to focus on the important facets of my life: family, spouse, children, friends, health, fun, and wealth.

This can have an amazingly powerful effect, and it is also very easy to do. Best of all, it takes only two minutes: 120 seconds.

Little actions like these can help us create good, balanced habits as well as break unhealthy one-dimensional habits.

Yogis follow basic life principles for creating balance. We can emulate them by being conscious of what we do each day and how we do it.

We can ask ourselves:

- Is what I am doing something that is worthwhile?

- Will it contribute to the happiness or well-being of someone else?

- Am I doing something that may touch another person's life positively?

We should take inventory of our thoughts, deliberately and carefully plan our actions, and make them purposeful.

It is also very important to have good intentions, and to know in our hearts that we have acted out of goodness and not selfishness.

Of course, even with the very best of intentions, there will be times in our lives when we un-intentionally hurt someone's feelings. When this happens, we should apologize as soon as possible.

People come from various backgrounds and families, and they will interpret our actions and words based upon their own experiences and life history. Even though we may have the best of intentions, others may interpret our actions in a different light.

We should not let that stop us from interacting with others, and stepping forward to lead. We should not be overly sensitive to criticism.

Realize that life is abundant. There is enough for everyone. Wish others well, be grateful, and let go of ill-will.

Think happy and positive thoughts. How can you do that? Make a list of happy events in your life and recall them vividly; anchor them in your brain. As you practice the art of visualization, create a picture of a happy and fulfilling future. Don't muddy the picture with worries of what may or may not happen. Simply expect the best out of life and see it with your mind's eye.

Take simple steps daily toward happiness. Identify the things that make you happy. Learn to tune into yourself and determine what catches your fancy in life. Surround yourself with those things. It is often the little things in life that add up to creating a happy and fulfilling life. Give heed to these factors in life.

I personally love listening to good music. I always carry my favorite music collection with me in the car or during my travels. As I enjoy my tea in the office, I pour the steaming hot tea into a beautiful china cup and saucer rather than a paper cup. The tea tastes better and the sight of the pretty flowers dancing on the cup soothes my soul. When I write a report, I pull out my beautiful Mont Blanc or Porsche Crest pen that I enjoy writing with. These pens write much better than the basic pens from the office supply room and the writing itself becomes a beautiful experience.

As you go through life, remember that everything you do, no matter how little or large, leaves a mark in your psyche and in those around you. So why not act in goodness, in love, and in joy? Balance your life between work and play, between career and family, between a job and health, and learn to enjoy life fully as you become the master of Yogi Power™.

Town of Ranchi, India:

The afternoon is bright with colors. The holiday drummers stretch out their arms and hit their drums in unison.

It is the celebration of "Holi" in the month of March: the festival of colors. There is a mythological story behind the celebration of Holi in India relating to a Prince who survived the pyre of fire in which the King tried to burn him. The contemporary significance of this day is rooted in forgiveness.

In India, this is the day when neighbors greet one another with hugs and kisses, forget old grudges, ill will, and caste aside hurt feelings.

My brother and I are running with the other children from one neighbor's house to the next, devouring the candies offered to us. We splash the "gulal" (colored celebratory powder) on each others cheeks and clothes, drowning ourselves in the beauty of the colors around us.

As the sun begins to dip down, we return to our homes, tired from the non-stop dancing, singing, and feasting, cleansed of all ill-will and every grudge.

We can each create a day of forgiveness in our lives, and in the lives of our families. We can reach out to others with love rather than wounded pride and egotistical selfishness. Ill will saps our energy and our strength. It weakens us.

We can also visualize what we want our lives to look like. As we practice meditation on a daily basis, we can go through the list of things we want in life:

- Love we want to give and receive.

- People we want in our lives.

- Success we see ourselves achieving.

We can do something small daily to achieve these goals. With each small action that we take, we will begin to notice how our dreams and goals begin to manifest in our lives.

BREATHE

BE STILL

SMILE

Directions for use:

Whenever you feel that stress, anger, or frustration is interfering with your ability to function optimally or whenever you begin to feel disconnected, disjointed, and disorganized, take 60 seconds to create your own little mental oasis, and follow three simple steps:

- **Breathe** – With eyes closed, draw in positive energy, and exhale negative energy. (Slow inhalations and slow exhalations, 20 seconds.)

- **Be still** – Go to the center of your being. (Sitting perfectly still, 20 seconds.)

- **Smile** – Turn all negativity, both internal and external, into positive energy. (Eyes still closed, counting silently to 20 in your mind.)

You can follow these steps as often as once an hour or whenever you feel the need for it. This secret EXECUTIVE YOGI technique can help you maximize your performance and your sense of well-being. Regard this as your own secret SIXTY SECOND mental oasis.

Index

INDEX

E

East Africa 155
Elegance 76, 90
Elephant 13, 15, 16, 19, 45
Employees 26, 34, 93, 94
Employer(s) 26, 94
Energy 10, 22, 23, 37, 49, 66, 69, 70, 74, 75, 82, 96, 97, 115, 116, 118,
    131, 141, 147, 159, 171, 172, 183, 195, 197
English Tea 168
Envelope 87, 120, 150
Ethics 152
Evaporated Canned Milk 168
Excuse(s) 46, 53, 80
Executive Yogi 10, 23, 37, 49, 66, 82, 97, 116, 141, 172, 183, 197
Exercise 52, 54, 56, 58-62, 64, 107
Exhalations 10, 20, 23, 37, 49, 66, 82, 96, 116, 141, 171, 183, 197

F

Fabric(s) 33, 86, 87, 105
Family xvii-xix, xxiii, xxiv, 28, 30, 53, 57, 58, 60, 64, 68, 70, 84, 104-
    106, 107, 110, 112, 113, 125, 138, 143-145, 157, 159-163, 170,
    174, 175, 177-180, 187, 190, 193, 207
Family Mission Statement 105
Fan 28
Father's Day 125
Feast 87, 103, 174, 195
Festival of Colors 194
Finances 106, 179
Fitness Equipment 53
Fitness Program 52
Flashlight 86, 146
Flowers 76, 87, 102, 121, 134, 157, 193
Focus 17-20, 26, 29, 72, 107, 109, 111, 124, 129, 158, 160, 190
Forgiveness 194, 195
Fresh Air 61
Friend(s) xiii, xvii, xxiv, 30, 57, 77, 78, 80, 85, 102-107, 109, 110, 113-
    115, 118-120, 128, 140, 175, 179, 187, 188, 190
Fritters 114
Fun 35, 53, 56, 58, 60, 65, 104, 137, 156, 159, 179, 190

INDEX

Q

Queen Mumtaz 88

R

Race 58, 151, 175
Resort 110, 164, 165
Responsibility 148, 149, 161, 162, 186
Rice Pilaf 175
Roller Skating 100
Rolodex 109
Rome 95

S

Sari 69, 87, 152
School 12, 13, 20, 55, 111, 158, 162, 169, 174-176, 187, 188
School Bus 55
Scrapbooks 107, 109
Sister 30, 101, 157, 158, 159
Son 104, 105, 108, 111, 147, 148, 155, 157, 158, 160, 161, 163, 167, 168
Spouse 93, 128, 129, 190
Stamp of Love 132
Star 186
Stillness 17, 18, 21
Stock Market 160
Story-Telling 152, 153
Stress 9, 22, 36, 49, 65, 78, 82, 96, 115, 141, 171, 183, 196
Summer 32, 100, 111
Sun Pose 61
Suryah Namaskar 61
Swing(ing) 56, 100

T

Taj Mahal xxiii, 88, 140, 207
Tanzania 155
Tea 4, 76, 77, 79, 80, 102, 114, 130, 131, 168, 169, 193
Teacher(s) 14, 15, 18, 29, 148, 187, 188, 189
Temple 4, 174, 175, 176, 177, 178
Torrance Memorial Hospital 77
Trunk 15, 85, 86

AUTHOR INFORMATION

You can contact the author,
Ms. Neeti Dewan via email at:
Neeti@TheExecutiveYogi.com

AUTHOR'S BIO

Neeti Dewan was born in Agra, India, home of the Taj Mahal. As a teenager she moved to Los Angeles, and is a graduate of California State University. A Certified Public Accountant, she has been the CEO of her own company and has worked for Fortune 500 companies like Aramark Corporation, British Petroleum, Hughes Electronics, and Big-4 accounting firms, Pricewaterhouse-Coopers and Arthur Andersen. Ms. Dewan lives with her family in the Los Angeles area. For more info, visit www.TheExecutiveYogi.com.

Book Order Form:

Please send _____ copy/copies at $22.95 each plus shipping. (see below)

For the quickest service go to www.TheExecutiveYogi.com click on "Order Now", complete the online order form, and push "submit!" Discounts are available on orders of more than 100 books.

Ship to: _____

Name: _____

Address: _____

City: _____ State: _____ Zip: _____

Sales tax: is added on products shipped to California.

U.S. Orders: $4.00 per book for shipping and handling. International Orders: $9.00 per book shipping and handling. (Note: shipping and handling charges are based on actual cost and are subject to change.)

Payment: _____ Check or _____ Credit Card

_____ VISA _____ MasterCard _____ AMEX

Card Number: _____

Name on card: _____

Expiration Date: _____

Address credit card bill is sent to: _____

City: _____ State: _____ Zip: _____